MARGO OLIVER'S
GOOD FOOD FOR ONE

Easy recipes for today's busy singles

Illustrations by Janette Lush

Self-Counsel Press
(*a division of*)
International Self-Counsel Press Ltd.
Canada   U.S.A.

Printed in Canada
First edition: October, 1990

Canadian Cataloguing in Publication Data
Oliver, Margo, 1923-
Margo Oliver's good food for one

(Self-counsel series)
ISBN 0-88908-889-6

1. Cookery for one.   I. Title.   II. Title:
Good food for one.   III. Series.
TX652.045   1990   641.5′61   C90-091495-5

Cover photo by Derik Murray Photography Inc., Vancouver

Self-Counsel Press
(*a division of*)
International Self-Counsel Press Ltd.
Head and Editorial Office
1481 Charlotte Road
North Vancouver, British Columbia V7J 1H1

U.S. Address
1704 N. State Street
Bellingham, Washington 98225

CONTENTS

PREFACE

Lucullus was a Roman general (c. 110 B.C. - 56 B.C.) who, when he retired, spent huge sums on an extravagant way of life. He hosted incredible meals — at incredible cost.

The story goes that once, tiring of all the people around him, he ordered his chef to prepare a meal for one. When the meal arrived, it was disappointing. The chef, summoned to explain, said that he didn't feel he needed to be so particular when his boss was dining alone.

At that, the great gourmet turned an icy eye on the chef and said that when he was alone there should have been special attention to the meal because then "Lucullus dines with Lucullus."

I say, "Hooray for Lucullus!" Remember him when you find yourself dining with you!

Seriously, there can be pleasures in eating with one's self. You can eat whatever appeals to you without considering the tastes of others. You can eat at whatever hour you choose. And you can eat any place you want — at your dining table, in your favorite chair, or even propped up in bed. But eating won't be a pleasure unless the food you offer you is nicely prepared and presented attractively.

Unfortunately, loners too often say, "I'm just not interested in cooking for myself." After a hard day's work and perhaps a frustrating journey home, it's so easy to collapse into a chair, feeling you just can't be bothered. Or, if you are a college student living away from home, cooking may seem too time-consuming when your evenings are filled with social activities as well as assignments. If you are older, you perhaps find that food just doesn't interest you even if you have the time.

Yet everyone knows that good, nourishing food is vitally important if you are to feel well. That's true, no matter what your age.

I lived alone for years before I married and now I live alone again. I *do* try to make sure I eat well every day. Of course, there are days when I don't want anything more than a simple salad. And I try to make things ahead for the times I just don't want to cook.

This book has been drawn from my own experience. I have offered some help in planning make-ahead meals and suggested recipes I hope you'll want to try simply because they sound so good, yet are relatively easy and quick to prepare. I hope to remind you that preparing good meals (even for you dining with you) should and can be interesting and fun!

THIS & THAT
▼▼▼

ABOUT COOKING AND BAKING UTENSILS

When you are cooking for one, it is a great help to have some small cooking dishes and pans. They are available in houseware departments and in kitchen stores. Some of my own particular favorites come from a local potter. I find foil pans quite useful except when I want something to brown well underneath. I have included metric as well as imperial measurements here to help you purchase exactly what you want.

The basic pans and baking dishes used in this book are these:

Foil pans:

5½ x 3¼ x 2-inch (14 x 8 x 5-cm) loaf pan

7½ x 4 x 2½-inch (19 x 10 x 6.5-cm) loaf pan

Baking dishes and casseroles:

6-oz. (175-mL) custard cups

2- to 2½-cup (approximately 500-mL) casserole

8 x 6 x 2-inch (20 x 15 x 5-cm) baking dish (This is approximate — use any small rectangular or oval baking dishes that measure near this size and hold from 2½ cups to 4 cups — or about 500 mL to 1L)

1-qt. (1-L) casserole

Pots:

Small skillet about 7½ inches (18 cm) in diameter

1

Medium skillet about 10 inches (24 cm) in diameter

Small and medium saucepans

Large saucepan or Dutch oven

Extras:

Small roasting pan with rack

Broiler pan

Wok (optional)

Don't forget: Glass ovenware should not be used under the broiler or browning unit of either a microwave or toaster oven.

ABOUT INGREDIENTS

Herbs and spices

I've used many different herbs and spices in these recipes. It's really interesting to use them all. However, they do lose their flavor over time, so try to buy small amounts in bulk food stores or share large containers with friends.

Dried leaf herbs

I prefer the whole herbs to the ground so all these recipes have been tested with dried leaf herbs.

Fresh or dried herbs

If you have fresh herbs, use them by all means. If the recipe calls for dried herbs, double the amount if using fresh.

Curry powder

Of course, ideally we should make our own curry powder to suit each dish. However, I have found the hot and mild English curry powders suit my taste quite well.

Fresh ground pepper

Equip yourself with a good pepper mill. Since many of us are cutting down on salt, fresh pepper adds a real zip to foods.

Fresh garlic and ginger

These have become so easily available in the last few years that I'm sure you usually have them on hand. Garlic should be kept in a pot that has openings (or even just a jar with the lid off), not in the refrigerator. If it's fresh and firm when you buy it, it should keep several weeks. I usually keep fresh ginger loose in the crisper of the refrigerator. I find that if I wrap it or put it in a plastic bag, it molds quickly. While the cut ends may dry out when it is stored loose, the rest stays fresh for at least two weeks.

Fresh parsley

Many people don't buy parsley because they feel it will go bad before they can use it up. Try this. Chop it while it's fresh, then store it in a jar in the freezer. It's fine for almost any recipe. Italian parsley is the one with the large flat leaf. It has a nice but stronger flavor than regular parsley.

Stock mixes

You'll notice I have used chicken, beef, and vegetable stock mixes in many recipes. Of course it would be nicer to replace the mixes with homemade stock, but I have suggested the mix because I hear so many people say they'd never make stock. The mix comes as a powder in a small can and keeps almost indefinitely. Like bouillon cubes, its big disadvantage is too much salt. I have, therefore, used only small amounts and have eliminated or cut down the salt in the recipes.

I'd still like to recommend that you make your own stock and there are recipes on pages 126 and 127. While you do have to be at home when you make it, it really requires very little work — and it's so good! A useful idea is to freeze some stock in ice cube trays, then store the cubes in a plastic bag in the freezer. When you need a little stock you just pop one or two of the cubes into the pan.

Light or low-fat dairy products

Even sour cream comes in "light" these days. It's a good idea to use these low-fat products and skim milk whenever possible.

Brown rice

Besides having a delicious nutty flavor, brown rice offers more protein, minerals, niacin, and vitamin E than white rice. It does have more calories, however.

Salad greens

I like to have a salad every day. I usually buy two kinds of greens, often leaf or butter lettuce and romaine, separate and wash them, drying them as well as possible. Then I pack them in a plastic bag with paper towels between the layers. I find they keep very well for a week when stored in the refrigerator this way.

ABOUT THE MICROWAVE

In my view, the microwave cooks fish perfectly to give it extraordinarily good flavor and texture, but I have to admit that I'm less enthusiastic about using it for meat and poultry. So while I've tried to include all types of conventional cooking in the main dishes section, I've also added microwave directions only where I thought they would be particularly useful. But there are many good small uses for the microwave, including heating last night's roast so it's nearly as good as freshly cooked, softening butter and cheese and cheese spreads, and frying bacon so it's virtually fat free. One of my favorite small uses is to dry fresh herbs.

Put between sheets of paper towel or paper napkin, herbs can be dried in about half a minute.

ABOUT PREPARATION AND COOKING TIMES

Although each recipe gives a preparation and cooking time, these are only guides. All of us work at different speeds (and have different interruptions) and, while some of us may be able to overlap several operations to speed up preparation, less experienced cooks need to do each step individually.

Cooking time can vary too. The appliances themselves may provide different heats because thermostats aren't always accurate, and house power varies from one time of day to another and even from one part of the country to another. Different wattages in microwaves may affect timing too. Always check your dish at the minimum suggested cooking time.

ABOUT SERVING SIZES

I've always found it difficult to judge just how many servings can be made from a dish and it's even harder when the dishes are for one rather than for six. Most of my suggested servings are quite generous, but obviously a young man could easily clean up one of my two-serving casseroles, while his grandmother might find even one serving too much for her.

A number of recipes make two servings, especially the soups and casseroles. Most of us are quite glad to have something to heat up in a hurry and, in any case, making one serving of soup isn't very practical.

ABOUT LEFTOVERS

In many places I have suggested how to use up leftovers. For example, after each roast I have listed recipes that use what you haven't been able to eat in one or two meals.

Another problem with recipes for one is that often only a part of a package or can is called for. What to do with the rest? I've tried, where possible, to include more than one recipe using small amounts. There are many recipes using part containers of canned tomatoes, yogurt, and sour cream, for example. And there is more than one recipe using things such as part cans of crab, beets, tomato sauce, whole kernel corn, etc.

MAIN DISHES
▼▼▼

MAIN DISHES
▼▼▼

I'm starting this book with recipes for entrées because I think that's the most difficult part of planning a meal for one. And since I believe it's very important to pamper oneself occasionally, I have included recipes that are fairly sophisticated for the times you want to celebrate. Why not Pork Normande (p. 44) or Shrimp and Cucumber (p. 93)? But, there are recipes for the days you need "comfort food" too. Shepherd's Pie (p. 34) is always a comfort to me.

Don't tell me you never have a roast because you don't want to eat it every day for a week! Of course you can have roast beef, a roast chicken, or even some roast turkey. Recipes for all of them are included here, followed by suggestions for using the leftovers in delicious ways. I hope you'll find such things as Freezer Meatballs (p.13), Four-in-One Chicken (p. 56) and Four-Way Turkey Breast (p. 74) especially useful.

By the way, I've included suggestions for vegetables and salads to serve with most dishes. I hope they'll be helpful too.

RIB ROAST OF BEEF

▼▼▼

1	small clove garlic, crushed
¼ tsp.	salt
	Generous grating fresh pepper
⅛ tsp.	dried leaf marjoram
1	Standing rib roast of beef (1 rib, about 2 lb.)
1	small onion, cut in half
½ cup	dry red wine

Preparation:
5 minutes
Cooking:
1 hour,
20 minutes

Heat oven to 500 °F. Have a small roasting pan ready. Combine garlic, salt, pepper, and marjoram and rub into fat side of meat. Set roast on bone in roasting pan (support with balls of foil if necessary). Put in oven and immediately reduce heat to 325 °F. Cook until brown, about 20 minutes, then remove from oven.

Add onion and wine to pan and return roast to oven. Cook 25 to 30 minutes per pound for medium-rare. To be sure, use a meat thermometer (140 °F for rare, 160 °F for medium, 170 °F for well done). Baste often during cooking. Put meat on a hot platter when done. Make Pan Gravy (p. 260). (If liquid in pan has dried up by end of cooking, add about ¼ cup red wine to pan and stir up all browned bits, then pour into container.)

To use leftovers

Leftover Beef Stroganoff (p. 30)

Hot Roast Beef Sandwich (p. 221)

CROSS RIB ROAST WITH SQUASH
▼▼▼

1 tbsp.	cooking oil
1	small cross rib or short rib roast (about 2 lb.)
1½ cups	water
½ tsp.	dried leaf savory
¼ tsp.	pepper
2	small onions, peeled
½	acorn squash, cut in 3 or 4 wedges and peeled
¼ tsp.	salt

Preparation:
5 minutes
Cooking:
2 hours,
45 minutes

Heat oil in large, heavy saucepan over medium-high heat. Add roast and brown well on all sides. Add water, savory, and pepper and bring to a boil. Reduce heat, cover, and simmer until meat is just getting tender, about 2 hours.

Add onions and squash to pan, pushing onions down into liquid as much as possible. Sprinkle in salt, cover and simmer until everything is tender, about 30 minutes. Then put meat on hot platter, lift vegetables out with a slotted spoon and put around meat. Keep hot. Make Kettle Gravy (p. 260).

To use leftovers

Raw Potato Hash (p. 31)

Mushroom Meat Pie (p. 32)

Shepherd's Pie (p. 34)

MAXIMUM FREEZER STORAGE TIMES

Meat

Roast, steaks, and chops	Beef — 12 months
	Lamb, veal — 9 months
	Pork — 6 months
Ground	Beef, lamb, veal — 4 months
	Pork — 3 months
Ham and bacon	— 1 month
Sausage	— 2 months
Prepared stews, casseroles	— 3 to 4 months

Poultry

Whole	— 12 months
Cut up	— 6 months
Giblets	— 6 months
Ground	— 2 months
Cooked	— 1 month

Fish and Seafood

Fish	Lean — 6 months
	Fat — 2 months
Shrimp, oysters, clams, scallops	— 3 months
Crab, lobster	— 2 months
Fruits	— 12 months
Bread	— 3 months

Be sure to use good freezer wraps. Heavy-duty aluminum foil, heavy plastic wrap, and made-for-the-freezer plastic bags and containers are best.

FREEZER MEATBALLS
▼▼▼

2 lb.	lean ground beef
1 cup	fine dry bread crumbs
½ cup	finely chopped onion
2	eggs
1 cup	milk
1 tsp.	salt
⅛ tsp.	pepper
⅛ tsp.	ground nutmeg
1 tsp.	Worcestershire sauce
2 tbsp.	cooking oil
2 tbsp.	flour
1	can (10 oz. or 248 mL size) beef consommé
1 cup	water

Preparation:
15 minutes
Cooking:
20 minutes

Combine first 9 ingredients in a bowl and mix well. The soft texture means that the finished meatballs will be extra tender. Shape into small balls, about 1 inch in diameter. (You should have about 80.) Don't worry if the meatballs aren't completely round.

Heat oil in large heavy skillet and brown meatballs, lifting them out as they brown.

Sprinkle flour into drippings left in skillet and stir to blend. (Add 1 tbsp. oil if skillet has gone dry.) Remove from heat and stir in consommé and water. Return to high heat and stir until boiling, slightly thickened, and smooth. Reduce heat and simmer 5 minutes. Remove from heat and cool. You will have about 2⅓ cups.

Divide meatballs into 4 small containers (about 20 in each). Divide gravy evenly, pouring about ½ cup into each container. Seal containers and freeze. Thaw meatballs and use for any of the following recipes, one container for each recipe. Each portion of meatballs makes one large serving or two smallish ones.

Note: You might want to check one meatball in the skillet you intend to brown them in before you add others. When I was testing, I found they stuck badly in my old "stick-proof" pan. But when I used my brand-new Teflon-lined pan, they browned well with no sticking.

I love to have these meatballs on hand. I make them on a weekend so that I have four simple yet interesting meals for days when time is very limited.

Although the cooking time for each of the variations is quite long, the preparation time is very short, so once you have the sauce simmering you can quietly sit and watch the news, sip a glass of wine, or read the paper, and in a very little while you'll have a good dinner ready. Serve any of these with salad and perhaps some French bread.

CURRIED MEATBALLS
▼▼▼

2 tsp.	**butter or margarine**
1 tsp.	**curry powder**
⅔ cup	**chopped peeled apple (1 small)**
⅔ cup	**canned tomatoes with liquid**
2 tbsp.	**seedless raisins**
1	**container Freezer Meatballs (p. 13), thawed**
	Hot cooked rice
	Chutney

Preparation:
5 minutes
Cooking:
36 minutes

Heat butter or margarine in medium saucepan. Add curry powder and cook gently 3 minutes. Add apple and stir over medium heat until soft, about 3 minutes. Add tomatoes and raisins, reduce heat, cover and simmer 15 minutes.

Add meatballs, cover and simmer until meatballs are hot, about 15 minutes. Serve with rice and chutney.

MEATBALLS STROGANOFF
▼▼▼

2 tsp.	butter or margarine
½	small garlic clove, minced
½ cup	sliced mushrooms (3 large)
2 tsp.	flour
	Dash pepper
⅓ cup	water
1	container Freezer Meatballs (p. 13), thawed
⅓ cup	light sour cream
2 tsp.	chopped parsley or fresh dill
	Hot cooked rice

Preparation:
5 minutes
Cooking:
22 minutes

Melt butter or margarine in a medium saucepan. Add garlic and mushrooms and cook gently 3 minutes, stirring. Sprinkle in flour and pepper, stir to blend, and remove from heat. Stir in water, return to heat and stir until boiling, thickened, and smooth.

Add meatballs, cover, and simmer, stirring occasionally, until meatballs are hot, about 15 minutes. Stir in sour cream and heat but do not boil. Sprinkle with parsley or dill and serve with rice.

CREOLE MEATBALLS
▼▼▼

1 tbsp.	olive oil
1	small piece bay leaf
1 tbsp.	chopped parsley
1 tsp.	chopped celery leaves
⅓ cup	chopped green pepper
⅓ cup	regular long grain rice
¼ tsp.	salt
	Dash Tabasco sauce
	Dash cayenne
1 cup	canned tomatoes
⅓ cup	water
1	container Freezer Meatballs (p. 13), thawed

Preparation:
10 minutes
Cooking:
47 minutes

Heat oil in medium saucepan and add bay leaf, parsley, celery leaves, and green pepper. Cook gently 5 minutes, stirring. Add rice and stir until rice browns lightly. Add salt, Tabasco, cayenne, tomatoes, and water. Bring to a boil, reduce heat, cover, and cook gently until rice is tender and most of liquid is absorbed, about 25 minutes. Add meatballs and simmer until everything is very hot, about 15 minutes.

MEATBALLS POLYNESIAN
▼▼▼

1 tsp.	cooking oil
1	small clove garlic, minced
1 tsp.	minced fresh ginger
¼ cup	water
¼ tsp.	chicken stock mix
1	container Freezer Meatballs (p. 13), thawed
1	small green pepper, cut in 1-inch squares
⅓ cup	drained pineapple chunks
1 tbsp.	cornstarch
1 tbsp.	sugar
2 tbsp.	pineapple juice
2 tbsp.	cider vinegar
1 tbsp.	soya sauce
1	small tomato, peeled, seeded, and chopped coarsely
	Hot cooked rice or noodles

Preparation:
10 minutes
Cooking:
25 minutes

Heat oil in a medium saucepan. Add garlic and ginger and cook gently 2 minutes. Add water, stock mix, and meatballs. Cover and simmer 15 minutes. Add green pepper and pineapple pieces, cover again, and simmer 5 minutes (green pepper should be crisp). Mix cornstarch and sugar in a small bowl. Stir in pineapple juice gradually, blending until smooth. Stir in vinegar and soya sauce. Stir into boiling liquid and continue stirring until thickened and clear. Add tomato pieces and serve immediately with rice or noodles.

18

CHEESE BURGER
▼▼▼

¼ lb.	ground beef
1 tbsp.	minced onion
¼ tsp.	garlic salt
1 tsp.	cooking oil
1	slice process cheese
1 tbsp.	chili sauce
	Hamburger bun (optional)

Preparation:
5 minutes
Cooking:
6 to 8 minutes

Combine meat, onion, and garlic salt and shape the mixture into two thin patties, about ¼ inch thick. Make the patties big enough to enclose the cheese slice.

Heat oil in a small skillet. Put one patty in the skillet and top it with the cheese slice and then a scant tablespoonful chili sauce. Add remaining patty and press the two together around the edge to seal.

Cook over medium heat until well browned on both sides, turning once. This will take 3 to 4 minutes a side.

Serve on a bun if desired, or put on hot dinner plate and serve with sliced tomato and cucumber.

BEEF PATTIES IN SWEET-SOUR SAUCE
▼▼▼

3 tbsp.	white vinegar
3 tbsp.	brown sugar
⅓ cup	water
1 tbsp.	soya sauce
4	pork sausages
¼ lb.	ground beef
¼ tsp.	salt
	Dash pepper
	Pinch dried leaf thyme
2 tsp.	cooking oil
1	small onion, thinly sliced
1 tsp.	cornstarch
1 tbsp.	cold water

Preparation:
10 minutes
Cooking:
40 minutes

Combine vinegar, brown sugar, ⅓ cup water, and soya sauce in a small bowl, stirring until sugar is dissolved.

Squeeze sausage meat out of the skins into another bowl. Add ground beef, salt, pepper, thyme, and 2 tsp. of the vinegar mixture. Blend well with a fork. Shape into two patties about 1 inch thick. Heat oil in a medium skillet. Add patties and brown slowly on both sides. Drain off fat, then add onion and remaining vinegar mixture. Cover tightly and simmer 30 minutes, turning patties several times. Lift meat patties onto hot serving plate. Combine cornstarch and 1 tbsp. water, stirring until smooth. Bring liquid in pan to a boil and stir enough of the cornstarch mixture into boiling liquid to thicken slightly. Reduce heat and simmer 3 minutes, stirring. Pour over meat.

CHEESE AND PICKLE MEAT LOAF
▼▼▼

1 lb.	lean ground beef
½ cup	quick-cooking rolled oats
1	egg
¾ cup	grated old cheddar cheese
⅓ cup	chili sauce
1	small onion, chopped
1	large dill pickle, chopped
2 tbsp.	dill pickle juice
½ tsp.	Worcestershire sauce
¼ tsp.	salt
¼ tsp.	black pepper

Preparation:
5 minutes
Cooking:
50 minutes

Heat oven to 350 °F. Grease two foil loaf pans, 5½ x 3¼ x 2 inch.

Combine all ingredients and pack into prepared pans. Wrap one loaf in aluminum foil and freeze to use another day. Bake the other loaf 50 minutes and serve hot or cold. When ready to use second loaf, thaw and bake in the same way.

Cut in thick slices to serve.

Try this served with Quick Scalloped Potatoes (p. 155) and Pepper Slaw (p. 181).

Makes 2 small loaves.

SKILLET SPAGHETTI
▼▼▼

1 tbsp.	olive oil
¼ lb.	ground beef
¼ cup	chopped onion
1	small clove garlic, minced
1	can (7½ oz. or 213 mL size) tomato sauce
1 cup	water (or ½ cup each water and red wine)
¾ tsp.	chili powder
¼ tsp.	salt
¼ tsp.	dried leaf basil
¼ tsp.	dried leaf oregano
¼ tsp.	sugar
	Dash pepper
1 cup	broken spaghetti
	Parmesan cheese

Preparation:
5 minutes
Cooking:
50 minutes

Heat oil in medium skillet. Add beef and brown lightly over medium heat, breaking it apart as it browns. Add onion and garlic and stir 2 minutes. Add all remaining ingredients except spaghetti and Parmesan cheese, bring to a boil, reduce heat and boil gently, uncovered, 30 minutes. Add spaghetti, reduce heat, cover, and simmer 15 minutes or until spaghetti is tender. Turn out onto hot plate and sprinkle with Parmesan cheese.

Serve with Garlic Bread (p. 213) and a tossed green salad. A glass of dry red wine is good too!

STEAK AND EGG
▼▼▼

¼ cup	canned tomato sauce
¼ cup	chopped green pepper
1 tbsp.	finely chopped onion
2 tsp.	lemon juice
2 tsp.	brown sugar
¼ tsp.	Worcestershire sauce
	Dash Tabasco sauce
⅛ tsp.	chili powder
	Pinch each celery seed, ground cinnamon, ground cloves
1 tbsp.	butter or margarine
1	minute steak (or cube steak)
1	egg
	Grating fresh pepper
1 tbsp.	grated old cheddar cheese

Preparation:
5 minutes
Cooking:
25 minutes

Combine tomato sauce, green pepper, onion, lemon juice, sugar, Worcestershire sauce, Tabasco sauce, chili powder, and spices in a small saucepan. Bring to a boil, reduce heat, and simmer 15 minutes, stirring occasionally. Keep hot.

Heat half the butter or margarine in a small heavy skillet over high heat. Fry steak quickly until nicely browned, 2 to 3 minutes a side. Put on hot serving plate and keep hot.

Add remaining butter to skillet and fry egg over medium-low heat until done as you like it, about 3 minutes. Add sauce to steak, then top with the egg and sprinkle egg with pepper and the cheese.

LEMON STEAK
▼▼▼

1½ tsp.	cooking oil
1 tbsp.	butter or margarine
¼ tsp.	dry mustard
1	small steak, about 6 oz. (strip loin, T-bone, wing), cut about ½ inch thick
	Grating fresh pepper
	Salt
1 tbsp.	lemon juice
2 tsp.	finely chopped parsley
1 tsp.	finely chopped chives
1 tsp.	Worcestershire sauce

Preparation:
5 minutes
Cooking:
5 minutes

Heat a small heavy skillet, just large enough to hold the steak.

Add the oil and half the butter or margarine. Stir in the mustard over high heat and add the steak. Sprinkle top side of steak with pepper, turn heat to medium-high, and cook 2 minutes. Turn and season second side lightly with salt and pepper. Cook 2 minutes longer. Put on hot serving plate.

Add lemon juice, remaining butter or margarine, parsley, chives, and Worcestershire sauce to skillet and stir to blend. Return steak to pan, turn over in pan liquid and heat over high heat for 30 seconds for medium-rare or until done the way you like it.

Serve with Stuffed Baked Potatoes (p. 152) and baked tomato.

STEAK WITH MUSTARD SAUCE
▼▼▼

1 tbsp.	butter or margarine
1 tbsp.	chopped green pepper
1 tbsp.	chopped onion
1½ tbsp.	Dijon mustard
¼ cup	consommé (or ¼ cup water and ¼ tsp. beef stock mix)
2 tsp.	cooking oil
1	minute steak, 4 to 6 oz. (sometimes called cube steak)

Preparation:
3 minutes
Cooking:
15 minutes

Melt butter or margarine in small saucepan. Add green pepper and onion and stir over medium heat 3 minutes. Stir in mustard and consommé (or water and stock mix) and cook over medium heat, stirring often, until slightly thickened, about 10 minutes.

Heat oil in a small, heavy skillet over medium-high heat and fry steak about 2 minutes a side. Add sauce and turn steak over in the sauce, then put it on a hot serving plate and pour the sauce over. Since the steak is quite mustardy, the gentle taste of mashed potatoes and a mild vegetable are a nice complement.

BEEF STRIPS IN ONION SAUCE
▼▼▼

¼ lb.	top round steak
1 tbsp.	flour
¼ tsp.	paprika
	Dash pepper
1 tbsp.	cooking oil
1 tbsp.	butter or margarine
¾ cup	chopped Spanish onion (½ medium)
¼ cup	chopped green pepper
½	small clove garlic, minced
2 tsp.	flour
¾ cup	water
¼ tsp.	beef stock mix
¼ tsp.	salt
	Dash pepper
	Pinch dried leaf savory
	Hot buttered noodles

Preparation:
10 minutes
Cooking:
15 minutes

Cut beef in thin strips across the grain. Mix 1 tbsp. flour, paprika, and dash pepper on waxed paper. Toss meat strips in mixture.

Heat oil in a heavy skillet over high heat. Add beef and cook quickly until lightly browned. Lift out with a slotted spoon and reduce heat to medium. Add butter or margarine to skillet.

Add onion, green pepper, and garlic and stir 3 minutes. Sprinkle in 2 tsp. flour and stir to blend. Remove from heat and stir in water and beef stock mix, salt, dash pepper, and savory.

Return to heat and bring to a boil, stirring constantly. Reduce heat and simmer 5 minutes. Add beef strips, cover, and simmer about 2 minutes or until meat is tender and hot. Taste and adjust seasoning if necessary.

Serve with noodles and add Marinated Vegetable Salad (p. 176).

BEEF AND SNOW PEAS
▼▼▼

¼ lb.	top round or sirloin steak, cut ½ inch thick
2 tsp.	cornstarch
2 tsp.	soya sauce
1 tsp.	cooking oil
20	snow peas (about 2 oz.)
1½ tbsp.	cooking oil
2 tbsp.	water

Preparation:
5 minutes
Cooking:
3½ minutes

Trim all fat from steak and discard. Cut steak in very thin strips across the grain. Put in a small bowl. Sprinkle with cornstarch and toss until cornstarch is mixed all through the meat. Pour soya sauce and 1 tsp. oil over meat and toss with a fork to blend.

Wash snow peas and break off ends, pulling off any strings. Heat ½ tbsp. of the oil to very hot in heavy skillet or wok. Add snow peas and cook over high heat 1 minute, stirring briskly. Lift out with a slotted spoon and keep hot (they should be bright green and crisp).

Add remaining 1 tbsp. oil to pan and heat to very hot. Add meat and cook over high heat 1 minute, stirring briskly. The meat should just lose its pink color — if it is overcooked it will be tough. Add water and return snow peas to pan. Cover and cook quickly 30 seconds, just to heat the peas. Serve immediately.

Serve with hot, cooked rice and Orange Salad (p. 194).

BEEF STROGANOFF
▼▼▼

1	filet mignon, about 6 oz.
½	clove garlic
1 tbsp.	flour
¼ tsp.	salt
	Dash pepper
1½ tbsp.	butter or margarine
2 tbsp.	finely chopped onion
½ cup	water
½ tsp.	beef stock mix
1 cup	sliced mushrooms
¼ cup	sour cream or plain yogurt
	Buttered noodles
	Snipped chives

Preparation:
10 minutes
Cooking:
25 minutes

Trim any fat from filet and rub all over with the cut side of the garlic. Mix flour, salt, and pepper and pound as much of the mixture as possible into the meat with the edge of a plate or a mallet. (The filet will end up being about 1 inch thick.) Save any leftover flour mixture. Cut meat into thin strips across the grain.

Heat butter or margarine in skillet over medium heat. Lightly brown the meat. Add onion and stir 2 minutes. Sprinkle in any leftover flour mixture and stir to blend. Remove from heat and stir in water and beef stock mix. Reduce heat and simmer 5 minutes, stirring often. Add mushrooms and continue simmering, uncovered, about 10 minutes, until meat is tender, adding a little water if necessary. Stir in sour cream or yogurt, heat (do not boil). Serve with noodles and sprinkle with chives.

29

LEFTOVER BEEF STROGANOFF
▼▼▼

½ cup	thin strips leftover roast beef
1 tbsp.	flour
1 tbsp.	butter or margarine
1	small onion, thinly sliced
1	small clove garlic, minced
½	can (10 oz. or 284 mL size) mushroom pieces, drained (about ½ cup)
¾ cup	water
1 tsp.	beef stock mix
1½ tsp.	tomato paste
	Generous grating fresh pepper
¼ tsp.	Worcestershire sauce
¼ cup	light sour cream

Preparation:
5 minutes
Cooking:
6 minutes

Cut beef strips about 1 inch wide, 3 inches long. Toss in flour (save any flour that is left). Heat butter or margarine in medium skillet and add meat, onion, garlic, and mushrooms. Stir over medium heat 3 minutes. Lift meat and vegetables out of pan with a slotted spoon and set aside. Stir leftover flour into drippings in pan, then remove from heat. Stir in water, beef stock mix, tomato paste, pepper, and Worcestershire sauce. Return to medium heat and stir until boiling, slightly thickened, and smooth. Add meat mixture and heat well. Stir in sour cream, heat (do not boil). Serve with hot buttered noodles and Herbed Peppers (p. 151).

RAW POTATO HASH
▼▼▼

½ cup	ground leftover roast (use any of beef, pork, lamb, or veal)
1¼ cups	coarsely grated raw potato (1 large — see note)
2 tbsp.	finely chopped onion
¼ cup	milk
¼ tsp.	salt
	Grating fresh pepper
2 tsp.	butter or margarine

Preparation:
5 minutes
Cooking:
45 minutes

Heat oven to 400°F. Butter a small casserole, 2 to 2½ cup size. Combine all ingredients except butter or margarine and turn into casserole. Dot with butter or margarine. Bake about 45 minutes or until potatoes are tender and crusty on top.

This makes a good lunch or supper, served with sliced tomatoes and Pepper Slaw (p. 181).

Note: Avoid new potatoes for this recipe — they are too gummy.

MUSHROOM MEAT PIE
▼▼▼

1 tbsp.	butter or margarine
1	small onion, chopped
1 cup	sliced fresh mushrooms
1 tbsp.	flour
¼ cup	thick leftover gravy
2 tbsp.	water
¾ cup	cubed leftover roast beef
¼ cup	cream-style cottage cheese
1 tbsp.	chopped parsley
¼ tsp.	salt
¼ tsp.	dried leaf marjoram or thyme
⅛ tsp.	pepper
½ cup	frozen peas (optional)
½ cup	packaged biscuit mix
2 tbsp.	milk

Preparation:
10 minutes
Cooking:
28 minutes

Heat oven to 425 °F. Grease a 1-qt. casserole.

Melt butter or margarine in medium saucepan. Add onion and mushrooms and cook quickly, stirring, 2 minutes. Sprinkle in flour and stir to blend. Remove from heat and stir in gravy, water, and meat. Return to medium heat and bring just to a boil, stirring constantly. Reduce heat, cover, and simmer 5 minutes.

Remove from heat and stir in cottage cheese, parsley, salt, marjoram or thyme, pepper, and peas. Turn into casserole.

Combine biscuit mix and milk in a small bowl, then beat with a fork for 30 seconds. Drop by small spoonfuls on top of meat mixture, making about 6 mounds.

Bake about 20 minutes, until biscuits are nicely browned and meat mixture is bubbling well. Good with tossed green salad.

Makes 2 servings.

To reheat in the microwave: Add 1 tbsp. water, cover tightly, and microwave at high 2 minutes. Turn ½ turn and microwave at high 2 minutes.

SHEPHERD'S PIE
▼▼▼

⅓ cup	leftover gravy
2 tbsp.	water
½ tsp.	Worcestershire sauce
	Generous pinch dried leaf savory
	Pinch ground nutmeg
½	small onion, chopped
1 cup	finely ground leftover roast beef
	Salt and pepper
2 tsp.	butter or margarine
1 tbsp.	light cream or milk
½ cup	leftover mashed potatoes (see note)
¼ tsp.	salt
1	egg white
1 tbsp.	chopped parsley
2 tsp.	butter or margarine

> **Preparation:**
> 10 minutes
> **Cooking:**
> 45 minutes

Heat gravy and water to boiling in a small saucepan. Stir in Worcestershire sauce, savory, nutmeg, and onion. Cover and simmer 10 minutes. Add meat and heat through. Mixture should be moist but not runny. Taste and add salt and pepper if needed.

Heat oven to 350°F. Butter a small casserole, 2 to 2½ cups in size. Heat 2 tsp. butter or margarine with cream or milk until butter is melted, then add to potatoes, beating until fluffy. Add ¼ tsp. salt and egg white and beat again. Stir in parsley.

Turn meat mixture into prepared casserole and spoon potato mixture on top. Dot with 2 tsp. butter or margarine.

Bake about 30 minutes or until potato is lightly browned and meat mixture is bubbling well. A nice accompaniment is Corn-Stuffed Tomato (p.158).

Note: If you don't have leftover potato, boil 1 medium potato and mash before beginning the rest of the preparation.

CORNED BEEF AND VEGETABLES
▼▼▼

4	small new potatoes, scrubbed but not peeled
2	small carrots, scraped and cut in half lengthwise
1	small onion, cut in half
1	small clove garlic
2	peppercorns
1	whole clove
1	small piece bay leaf
1 cup	water
¼ tsp.	beef or vegetable stock mix
1	small wedge cabbage
½	can (12 oz. or 340 g size) corned beef

> **Preparation:**
> 8 minutes
> **Cooking:**
> 30 minutes

Put potatoes, carrots, onion, garlic, peppercorns, clove, and bay leaf in a medium saucepan. Add the water and stock mix. Bring to a boil, cover, reduce heat, and cook about 15 minutes or until vegetables are nearly tender. Add cabbage wedge.

Put corned beef in a sieve, set over the simmering vegetables, and cover. Continue cooking 15 minutes or until all vegetables are tender and corned beef is hot. Put meat and vegetables on hot serving plate. Thicken the cooking liquid a little by combining 1½ tsp. flour with 1 tbsp. cold water and stirring the mixture into the boiling liquid. Strain over the meat and vegetables.

MINTY DEVILLED LAMB CHOPS
▼▼▼

2	thick loin lamb chops
2 tsp.	Worcestershire sauce
2 tsp.	butter or margarine
2 tsp.	lemon juice
2 tsp.	dry vermouth
	Grating fresh pepper
2 tbsp.	mint jelly
1 tsp.	white vinegar

Preparation:
35 minutes
including standing
time
Cooking:
16 to 20 minutes

Trim excess fat from chops and put them in a shallow dish.

Heat Worcestershire sauce, butter or margarine, lemon juice, vermouth, and pepper in a small saucepan just until butter or margarine is melted. Pour over chops, turn chops, and let stand at room temperature 30 minutes (or in refrigerator all day). Turn occasionally if possible.

Put chops on rack in broiler pan and broil low under the heat source 8 to 10 minutes a side or until done. Check doneness by cutting into meat near the bone with the point of a knife.

Heat marinade in a small saucepan shortly before chops are done. Add jelly and vinegar and heat gently until jelly is melted. Serve hot over chops. Good served with Mushroom Pilaf (p. 167) and Chopped Tomato Salad (p. 178).

CURRIED LAMB CHOPS
▼▼▼

2	loin lamb chops
2 tsp.	cooking oil
¼ cup	chopped onion
¼ cup	chopped peeled apple
2 tsp.	curry powder
2 tsp.	flour
¼ tsp.	salt
½ tsp.	sugar
⅛ tsp.	dry mustard
⅔ cup	chicken stock (p. 126)
1 tbsp.	lemon juice
	Hot cooked rice
	Chutney

Preparation:
5 minutes
Cooking:
40 minutes

Trim all excess fat from chops. Heat oil in medium skillet and brown the chops over medium heat. Set chops aside. Add onion and apple to oil left in skillet and stir 2 minutes. Sprinkle in curry powder and stir over low heat 1 minute. Sprinkle in flour, salt, sugar, and mustard and stir to blend. Remove from heat and stir in chicken stock and lemon juice. Return to high heat and bring to a boil, reduce heat, add chops, cover, and simmer about 30 minutes or until chops are very tender, turning after 15 minutes. Add a little water if the liquid is cooking away too much. Serve with rice and chutney and Cucumber Salad (p. 174).

Note: Use ⅔ cup water and ½ tsp. chicken stock mix in place of stock if desired.

ROAST LOIN OF PORK
▼▼▼

1	**2 to 2½ lb.**
	loin of pork (bone in)
	Olive oil
	Grating fresh pepper
	Dried leaf rosemary
1	**small clove garlic,**
	slivered (optional)
1 or 2	**medium potatoes,**
	peeled and cut in half

Preparation:
5 minutes
Cooking:
2 hours

Heat oven to 325 °F. Put roast on its bones in a small roasting pan. Rub all over with a little olive oil, then sprinkle generously with pepper and rosemary. Insert slivers of garlic into the roast in several places.

Roast about 2 hours or until meat thermometer registers 170 °F. Put potatoes around roast for last hour.

Put roast on hot platter and return potatoes to oven. Increase oven temperature to 400 °F to brown potatoes well, about 10 minutes. Put potatoes on platter with roast and make Pan Gravy (p. 260) with pan drippings if desired. Serve with applesauce and Celery and Corn in Sauce (p. 142). You can serve the roast hot for two meals if you have a microwave.

To use leftovers

Barbecued Pork Slices (p. 45)

Curried Pork and Rice (p. 46)

EASY PORK CHOP BAKE
▼▼▼

1	pork chop, about ¾ inch thick
1 tsp.	brown sugar
¼ tsp.	dried leaf rosemary
1½ tsp.	ketchup
1	thin slice onion
1	thin slice lemon

Preparation: 5 minutes
Cooking: 1 hour
Microwave: 25 minutes

Heat oven to 375 °F. Have ready a small baking dish just large enough to hold the chop.

Trim all excess fat from chop and put it in the baking dish. Mix brown sugar, rosemary, and ketchup and spread over chop. Top with onion slice, then lemon slice. Cover and bake about 1 hour or until chop is fork tender. Good with baked potato and steamed broccoli.

To microwave: Cover baking dish with plastic wrap and vent one corner. Microwave at medium about 25 minutes, turning ½ turn after 10 minutes. Let stand 5 minutes.

PORK STRIPS AND BEANS

1	thick loin pork chop
1 tsp.	cooking oil
1	thin slice fresh ginger
1	small clove garlic, peeled and cut in half
1 cup	fresh green beans, trimmed and cut in 1-inch pieces
2 tsp.	dry sherry
2 tsp.	soya sauce
¼ tsp.	sugar
2 tbsp.	water

Preparation:
7 minutes
Cooking:
9 minutes

Cut meat from chop bone, trim away all fat, and cut the meat into very thin strips across the grain.

Heat oil in heavy skillet or wok until very hot. Add ginger, garlic, and pork and stir constantly over high heat 2 minutes or until pork has lost all pink color. Lift meat out and keep hot. Leave ginger and garlic in pan. Add beans, sherry, soya sauce, sugar, and water. Stir to blend, cover tightly, and cook over medium heat about 5 minutes or until beans are tender-crisp. Stir occasionally and add a little more water if necessary. Return meat to pan and cook over high heat 30 seconds, stirring. Discard ginger and garlic. Serve immediately with hot buttered noodles and Glazed Baby Carrots (p. 140).

Note: This works well using fresh asparagus in place of the beans.

PORK TENDERLOIN WITH SPINACH
▼▼▼

1 tbsp.	flour
	Dash each salt and pepper
	Dash paprika
2	frenched slices pork tenderloin, about ¼ inch thick
1 tbsp.	cooking oil
1 tbsp.	margarine
1 tbsp.	flour
⅛ tsp.	salt
	Dash pepper
	Dash ground nutmeg
½ cup	2% milk
1	egg yolk
2 cups	fresh spinach (see note)
2 tbsp.	grated Swiss cheese

Preparation:
10 minutes
Cooking:
25 minutes

Combine 1 tbsp. flour and a dash each salt, pepper, and paprika on a piece of waxed paper. Dip tenderloin pieces into mixture to coat both sides. Heat cooking oil in small heavy skillet and fry tenderloin quickly to brown well. Reduce heat, cover pan, and cook gently until meat is tender, about 20 minutes. Keep hot.

While meat is cooking, melt margarine in small saucepan. Sprinkle in 1 tbsp. flour, ⅛ tsp. salt, dash pepper, and nutmeg and stir to blend. Remove from heat and stir in milk. Return to medium heat and stir until boiling, thickened, and smooth. Beat about half the hot sauce into the egg yolk gradually with a fork, then stir back into sauce. Bring just to the boiling point, turn heat to low and keep hot.

Heat oven to 450 °F. Have ready a small shallow baking dish.

Cook spinach in water clinging to leaves after washing (about 3 minutes). Drain, then chop by snipping with kitchen shears. Add 2 tbsp. of the thick hot sauce to the hot cooked spinach and spread the spinach in the baking dish. Top with the pork slices. Pour remaining sauce over all and sprinkle with cheese. Bake about 5 minutes or just until cheese is melted. Good served with hot cooked rice and Mushroom-Snow Pea Salad (p. 177).

Note: Pull tough stems out of spinach leaves and pack leaves lightly in cup to measure.

FRENCHED TENDERLOIN

Frenched pork tenderloin is usually available in any supermarket or butcher shop. It is simply a thick piece of whole tenderloin, cut across the grain and flattened.

If you buy a whole tenderloin rather than individual slices, you can french it yourself. Cut it into pieces about 2 inches (5 cm) long across the grain, set these pieces on one of the cut sides and flatten the meat by pounding with the flat of a cleaver, a rolling pin, or a mallet to the desired thickness. Extra slices can be frozen to use in other dishes.

PORK NORMANDE
▼▼▼

1½ tbsp.	butter or margarine
2	frenched slices pork tenderloin, about ¼ inch thick
2	thin slices onion
1	small Delicious apple, peeled and cored
1 tsp.	flour
¼ cup	apple cider or apple juice
2 tbsp.	water
½ tsp.	chicken stock mix
	Dash each salt and pepper
2 tsp.	Calvados or brandy (optional)
1 tbsp.	Crème Fraîche (p. 255) or drained plain yogurt

Preparation:
5 minutes
Cooking:
32 to 42 minutes

Heat butter or margarine in a small heavy skillet over medium heat. Add pork and brown slowly on both sides. Lift out and set aside. Add onion to pan and stir over medium-low heat 3 minutes. Slice apple into pan and stir 2 minutes. Sprinkle in flour and stir to blend.

Remove pan from heat and stir in apple cider or juice, water, stock mix, salt, and pepper. Return to heat and stir until boiling, slightly thickened, and smooth. Return meat to pan, cover, and simmer 30 minutes, turning once, or until meat is fork tender.

Put meat on hot serving plate and stir Calvados or brandy and Crème Fraîche or yogurt into sauce in skillet. Pour over meat.

BARBECUED PORK SLICES
▼▼▼

2	thin slices cold roast pork
1 tbsp.	cooking oil
1 tbsp.	finely chopped onion
2 tbsp.	tomato juice
2 tbsp.	ketchup
1 tbsp.	cider vinegar
2 tsp.	brown sugar
½ tsp.	Worcestershire sauce
⅛ tsp.	dry mustard
⅛ tsp.	chili powder
	Dash salt

Preparation:
5 minutes
Cooking:
18 minutes
Microwave:
9 minutes

Heat oven to 350 °F. Put pork slices in small individual baking dish.

Heat oil in small saucepan and add onion. Cook gently, stirring, 3 minutes. Add all remaining ingredients, bring to a boil, reduce heat, and simmer 5 minutes. Stir occasionally. Pour sauce over pork slices, cover, and heat in oven 10 minutes.

To microwave: Put pork slices on serving plate. Make sauce as above and pour over meat. Cover with transparent wrap, and heat in microwave on high 1 minute.

Serve with boiled potatoes and Golden Slaw (p. 180).

45

CURRIED PORK AND RICE
▼▼▼

2 tsp.	cooking oil
1	small onion, chopped
½ - ¾ tsp.	curry powder
¾ cup	cubed leftover pork roast
¾ cup	water
¼ tsp.	chicken stock mix
¼ cup	regular long grain rice
2 tbsp.	seedless raisins
1 tsp.	lemon juice
¼ tsp.	salt

Preparation:
5 minutes
Cooking:
30 minutes

Heat oil in medium saucepan. Add onion and curry powder and cook over medium heat 1 minute, stirring. Add meat and continue stirring until meat browns lightly, about 2 minutes.

Stir in remaining ingredients, bring to a boil, cover, reduce heat, and simmer 25 minutes or until rice is tender and water is absorbed.

Serve with chutney and tossed green salad.

SIMMERED COTTAGE ROLL
▼▼▼

2 to 2½ lb.	sweet pickled pork cottage roll
1	clove garlic, cut in half
1	bay leaf
4	whole cloves
1	small onion, quartered

Preparation:
5 minutes
Cooking:
1½ hours
Glazing:
20 minutes

Remove any outer wrapping on cottage roll and put meat in a large deep saucepan or Dutch oven. Add all remaining ingredients and cover with water. Bring to a boil, reduce heat and simmer about 1½ hours or until very tender and meat thermometer registers 170 °F.

If you wish, glaze (see Spicy Ham Glaze p. 256).

Serve the cottage roll hot for the first meal, then have some sliced cold for a second meal.

To use leftovers

Ham and Egg Salad (p. 185)

Ham and Cheese Spread (p. 214)

French-Toasted Ham Sandwich (p. 222)

BAKED BACK BACON
▼▼▼

1½ lb.	pickled back bacon in one piece
6	whole cloves
¼ cup	brown sugar
½ tsp.	dry mustard
2 tbsp.	sweet pickle liquid or pineapple juice

Preparation:
3 minutes
Cooking:
about 1½ hours

Heat oven to 350 °F. Put bacon on a large piece of heavy-duty aluminum foil and turn edge of foil up around meat. Score fat on bacon and stud with cloves. Combine remaining ingredients and drizzle over meat, then wrap foil securely around it. Put in small roasting pan and roast 1½ hours or until meat is very tender. Open foil for last 15 minutes of cooking and baste often to glaze. Meat thermometer will register 170 °F when bacon is done.

Serve bacon hot for first meal. You will need to slice it fairly thick. Once it is cold it is best sliced thin and it makes wonderful sandwiches. It can, of course, be used for any of the dishes suggested for leftover cottage roll and it is very good slivered to add to Chef's Salad (p. 172).

HAM AND SWEET POTATO
▼▼▼

1	medium sweet potato
1	small slice ready-to-eat ham, cut ¾ inch thick
1 tbsp.	brown sugar
⅓ cup	orange juice
1 tbsp.	lemon juice
1 tbsp.	liquid honey
	Orange sections (optional)

> **Preparation:**
> 15 minutes
> **Cooking:**
> 30 to 45 minutes
> **Microwave:**
> 17 minutes

Boil sweet potato 10 minutes or just until a fork will penetrate about ¼ inch. Cool until you can handle it, then peel and cut in thick slices. Heat oven to 350 °F. Have ready a shallow baking dish just large enough to hold the ham slice. Trim ham and put in baking dish. Sprinkle with brown sugar and top with sweet potato slices. Combine orange juice, lemon juice, and honey and pour over. Cover and bake 30 to 45 minutes, basting often, until potato is tender. Uncover for last few minutes of cooking.

To microwave: Prick sweet potato in several places with the tines of a fork and put in the microwave at high for 2 minutes. Let stand 5 minutes, then peel and slice as above.

Put 1 tbsp. water in dish. Add ham, sprinkle with sugar, and top with sweet potato. Cover and microwave at high 8 minutes. Add mixture of juices and honey, cover, and microwave at medium 7 minutes or until potato is tender, basting twice. Garnish with orange sections and serve with green beans.

ASPARAGUS-CHEESE BAKE
▼▼▼

4	stalks fresh asparagus
2	slices packaged cooked ham
1 tbsp.	butter or margarine
2 tsp.	flour
¼ tsp.	dry mustard
⅓ cup	skim milk
	Dash Worcestershire sauce
¼ cup	grated old cheddar cheese
1 tbsp.	grated old cheddar cheese
2	slices whole wheat toast

Preparation:
10 minutes
Cooking:
20 minutes

Heat oven to 350 °F.

Trim asparagus and cook about 5 minutes or until just beginning to get tender. Roll 2 stalks in each piece of ham and put in a small greased baking dish. Heat butter or margarine in a small saucepan, sprinkle in flour and mustard, and stir to blend. Remove from heat and stir in milk and Worcestershire sauce. Return to heat and stir until boiling, thickened, and smooth. Stir in ¼ cup cheese. Pour over ham rolls and sprinkle with 1 tbsp. cheese. Heat in oven until bubbly, about 10 minutes. Serve on toast for a weekend lunch. Add a fruit salad, perhaps Confetti Salad (p. 195).

SAUSAGE AND MACARONI SKILLET
▼▼▼

4	**pork sausages**
½	**small onion, chopped**
¼ cup	**chopped green pepper**
¼ cup	**chopped celery**
1 cup	**canned tomatoes, with juice**
¼ cup	**uncooked elbow macaroni**
¼ cup	**water**
	Pinch each sugar and salt
	Grating fresh pepper
¼ tsp.	**dried dill weed or ½ tsp. snipped fresh dill**
⅓ cup	**plain yogurt**

Preparation:
10 minutes
Cooking:
45 minutes

Squeeze sausage meat out of casings into a medium-size heavy skillet. Stir meat, breaking it apart, over medium heat until lightly browned, about 10 minutes.

Pour off almost all fat and add onion, green pepper, and celery. Stir 3 minutes, then add remaining ingredients, except yogurt. Break up tomatoes with a wooden spoon, bring mixture to a boil, reduce heat, cover, and simmer 30 minutes, stirring occasionally.

Stir in yogurt and heat but do not boil. Serve immediately.

This will make a generous lunch or supper. Serve with Golden Slaw (p. 180).

51

VEAL PICCATA

¼ lb.	veal cutlet, ¼ inch thick
	Salt and pepper
2 tsp.	lemon juice
1 tsp.	flour
1 tbsp.	butter
2 tbsp.	dry sherry
1 tbsp.	water

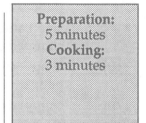

Preparation:
5 minutes
Cooking:
3 minutes

Trim any fat and sinew from veal, then pound the meat between two sheets of waxed paper with a mallet, the side of a cleaver, or a rolling pin until as thin as possible (⅛ to ¹⁄₁₆ inch thick). Cut into strips approximately 4 inches long by 1 inch wide.

Season veal with salt and pepper and drizzle with lemon juice. Dust lightly with flour.

Heat butter in small heavy skillet. Fry pieces of veal quickly 1 minute a side. Lift the strips out as they brown. Add sherry and water to pan and bring to a boil, stirring up any browned bits. Return meat to pan and heat 30 seconds. Serve with brown rice and Buttered Celery and Onion (p. 143).

VEAL AND MUSHROOMS

1	veal cutlet, ¼ inch thick
1 tbsp.	commercial French dressing
1 tbsp.	cooking oil
1	thin slice onion, separated into rings
1 tsp.	flour
	Salt and pepper
1 tbsp.	finely chopped green pepper
⅓ cup	boiling water
¼ tsp.	chicken stock mix
2 tsp.	butter or margarine
½ cup	sliced fresh mushrooms
1 tbsp.	sliced stuffed olives

Preparation:
7 minutes
Cooking:
12 minutes
Standing:
15 minutes

Pound veal between two sheets of waxed paper with the side of a cleaver or a rolling pin to ⅛ inch thick. Coat the veal with French dressing and let stand at room temperature 15 minutes.

Heat oil in medium skillet, shake excess dressing from cutlet, and brown meat lightly in oil. Push meat to one side of pan and add onion rings to other side. Cook gently 3 minutes, stirring. Sprinkle flour over onions and stir to blend. Push meat back into center of pan and sprinkle lightly with salt and pepper. Add green pepper, boiling water, and stock mix. Cover tightly and cook gently about 5 minutes a side or until veal is very tender.

Heat butter or margarine in another skillet while veal is cooking. Add mushrooms and cook quickly 3 minutes, stirring. Remove from heat. Put veal on hot serving plate. Turn mushrooms into liquid left in veal cooking pan. Add olives, stir, and heat well. Pour over veal.

Serve with Stuffed Baked Potato (p. 152) and tossed green salad.

ROAST CHICKEN
▼▼▼

1	3 to 4 lb. chicken
	Pepper
	Sage, savory, or poultry seasoning
1	small onion, cut in half
1	large sprig celery leaves
1	sprig parsley
1	slice lemon
	Olive oil or soft margarine

Preparation:
10 minutes
Cooking:
about 1½ hours

Rinse chicken inside and out and pat dry with paper towels. Heat oven to 325 °F. Have ready a small roasting pan with a rack. Sprinkle inside of chicken generously with pepper, then with one of the other herbs. Add onion, celery leaves, parsley, and lemon. Tie legs close to body, tuck tail into cavity, and bend the wings under the back. Put chicken on rack in roasting pan, breast side up. Brush with olive oil or rub with soft margarine. Cover loosely with foil.

Roast about 1½ hours or until juices run clear and the meat is fork-tender. Remove foil after ¾ hour. Put chicken on a warm platter and let stand a few minutes before carving. If desired, make Pan Gravy (p. 260).

Note: Giblets and neck can be simmered ahead of time to make liquid for gravy.

To use leftovers

California Chicken Almond (p. 68)

Creamed Chicken on Toast (p. 70)

FOUR-IN-ONE CHICKEN

Here's a way to use a small chicken for three main dishes and a stock.

3 to 3½ lb. fresh chicken cut into:

2	**sides of breast, boned**
2	**wings, tips removed**
2	**legs, separated into thighs and drumsticks**
	back, neck, and giblets

Freeze what you're not going to use immediately in separate packages, this way:

2	**sides of breast in first package**
2	**thighs and 1 drumstick in a second package**
2	**wings and 1 drumstick in a third package**
	Bones from breast, the back, neck, giblets, and wing tips in a fourth package

Mark each package and use as desired for Glazed Curry Chicken (p. 57), Coated Chicken Breast (p. 58), Chicken Skillet Dinner (p. 59), Chicken Stock (p. 126), or any of the other recipes in this section calling for chicken pieces.

GLAZED CURRY CHICKEN
▼▼▼

2	chicken thighs and 1 drumstick (see Four-in-One Chicken p. 56)
	Salt and pepper
1 tsp.	cooking oil
1	slice bacon, chopped finely
¼ cup	finely chopped onion
1 tsp.	curry powder
2 tsp.	flour
⅓ cup	chicken stock (p. 126)
1 tbsp.	orange marmalade
2 tsp.	ketchup
2 tsp.	lemon juice

Preparation:
10 minutes
Cooking:
45 to 50
minutes

Thaw chicken pieces if frozen. Heat oven to 400°F. Have ready a small baking dish about 8 x 6 x 2 inches. Sprinkle chicken lightly with salt and pepper and rub with oil on all sides. Put in baking dish and bake 30 minutes.

Put bacon and onion in a small skillet and stir over medium heat 3 minutes. Sprinkle in curry powder and stir 1 minute. Sprinkle in flour and stir to blend. Remove from heat and stir in stock. Return to heat and stir until boiling, thickened, and smooth. Mix in remaining ingredients and pour over chicken. Continue baking until chicken is tender and glazed, 15 to 20 minutes.

Note: Use ⅓ cup water and ¼ tsp. chicken stock mix in place of stock if desired.

COATED CHICKEN BREAST
▼▼▼

2 sides	chicken breast, boned (see Four-in-One Chicken p. 56)
1 tbsp.	flour
¼ cup	plain yogurt
	Pinch each sage, thyme, and basil
¼ tsp.	salt
	Dash pepper
1 tsp.	grated onion
¼ tsp.	lemon juice
⅓ cup	fine cracker crumbs
3 tbsp.	grated cheddar cheese
¼ tsp.	paprika

Preparation:
5 minutes
Cooking:
45 minutes

Thaw chicken if frozen. Heat oven to 350°F. Butter a small baking dish, about 8 x 6 x 2 inches.

Sprinkle chicken pieces with flour to lightly coat both sides. Combine yogurt, seasonings, onion, and lemon juice in a flat dish. Combine crumbs, cheese, and paprika in another flat dish.

Dip chicken in yogurt mixture, then in crumb mixture to coat both sides. Put in baking dish, cover, and bake 30 minutes. Uncover and bake until tender, about 15 minutes more.

58

CHICKEN SKILLET DINNER
▼▼▼

2	chicken wings and 1 drumstick (see Four-in-One Chicken p. 56)
1	small sweet potato
2 tbsp.	flour
½ tsp.	salt
	Dash each pepper and paprika
2 tbsp.	cooking oil
1	small onion, sliced
1	small orange
¼ cup	slivered green pepper

Preparation:
30 minutes
Cooking:
35 minutes

Thaw chicken if frozen. Scrub sweet potato and cover with boiling water in a small saucepan. Boil until tender, about 30 minutes. Peel and slice in half lengthwise.

Combine flour, salt, pepper, and paprika in a flat dish and roll chicken in mixture to coat all sides. Heat oil in a medium skillet over medium heat, add chicken and brown lightly. Lift chicken out of pan, add onion to oil left in pan, stir 3 minutes, then return chicken to pan.

Cut 3 thin slices from center of unpeeled orange and set aside. Squeeze remaining orange, measure juice, and add water to make ½ cup liquid. Add to skillet, cover, and simmer 20 minutes.

Push chicken to one side of pan and add sweet potato to other side of pan. Sprinkle in green pepper and top chicken with orange slices. Cover and cook until everything is tender and hot, about 10 minutes.

59

FIVE-SPICE CHICKEN
▼▼▼

2 tbsp.	soya sauce
1 tbsp.	finely minced onion
1	small clove garlic, crushed
¼ tsp.	finely chopped fresh ginger
1	chicken leg, separated into drumstick and thigh (about 8 oz.)
⅛ tsp.	ground cinnamon
	Pinch ground allspice
	Pinch anise seeds, crushed between fingers
	Dash cloves
	Dash pepper

> **Preparation:**
> 5 minutes
> **Cooking:**
> 45 minutes
> **Marinating:**
> several hours

Combine soya sauce, onion, garlic, and ginger in a shallow baking dish, about 8 x 6 x 2 inches. Add chicken pieces, cover, and marinate in refrigerator 3 or 4 hours (or more), turning pieces once or twice.

Heat oven to 325 °F. Lift chicken out of marinade and set aside while you pour marinade into a small container and wipe out baking dish. Oil baking dish lightly and put chicken into dish. Mix spices and sprinkle over chicken. Bake 30 minutes, brushing with marinade occasionally. Turn and bake about 15 minutes more or until chicken is very tender.

Try Chopped Tomato Salad (p. 178) with this.

CHICKEN IN WINE
▼▼▼

1	chicken leg, separated into drumstick and thigh
1 tbsp.	flour
	Dash each salt and pepper
¼ tsp.	paprika
1	strip bacon, diced
1 tbsp.	olive oil or margarine
1	small onion, cut in half
1	small clove garlic, cut in half
¼ cup	sliced mushrooms
½ cup	dry red wine
1	small piece bay leaf
	Pinch dried leaf thyme
2 tsp.	chopped parsley

Preparation:
10 minutes
Cooking:
1 hour,
15 minutes

Heat oven to 350 °F. Have ready a small baking dish, about 8 x 6 x 2 inches. Skin chicken pieces and roll in a mixture of flour, salt, pepper, and paprika. Fry bacon in medium skillet until done but not crisp. Drain on paper towelling and put in baking dish. Discard bacon fat and add olive oil or margarine to skillet. Add chicken pieces and brown lightly over medium heat. Lift chicken out as it browns, put it into baking dish. Add onion, garlic, and mushrooms to fat left in pan and stir 2 minutes over medium heat. Discard garlic. Add wine, bay leaf, thyme, and parsley and simmer 3 minutes. Pour over chicken, cover, and bake 1 hour, turning pieces after 30 minutes. Uncover and continue baking until very tender, about 15 minutes more.

CHICKEN AND PEPPERS
▼▼▼

½	small chicken breast
1 tsp.	cornstarch
2 tsp.	sherry
	Dash salt
2 tsp.	cooking oil
1 tsp.	cooking oil
½ cup	1-inch squares green pepper
¼ cup	diagonally sliced celery
	Very small pinch crushed dry red peppers
2 tsp.	water
	Pinch sugar
	Dash salt
2 tbsp.	sliced water chestnuts

Preparation:
10 minutes
Cooking:
4 minutes

Bone and skin chicken breast and cut meat into 1-inch squares. Combine cornstarch, sherry, and dash salt and pour over chicken pieces, tossing with a fork to coat chicken well.

Heat 2 tsp. oil in heavy skillet or wok, add chicken pieces and cook over high heat 2 minutes, stirring briskly. Lift out with a slotted spoon and keep hot. Add 1 tsp. oil to pan. Add green pepper, celery, and crushed dry red peppers. Cook over high heat 1 minute, stirring. Add water, sugar, dash salt, and water chestnuts. Cover tightly and cook quickly 30 seconds. Remove cover, add chicken pieces, and stir 30 seconds. Serve immediately with rice or noodles and steamed broccoli or asparagus.

KOREAN CHICKEN
▼▼▼

2 tbsp.	peanut oil
¼ cup	soya sauce
1 tbsp.	liquid honey
½	small clove garlic, finely chopped
⅛ tsp.	ground ginger
⅛ tsp.	dry mustard
1 tbsp.	chopped chives
2	chicken thighs
	Hot cooked noodles

Preparation:
5 minutes
Cooking:
45 minutes
Marinating:
several hours

Combine oil, soya sauce, honey, garlic, ginger, mustard, and chives in a shallow glass or pottery baking dish large enough to hold the chicken pieces. Add chicken and marinate several hours, turning once or twice. Heat oven to 425°F. Bake chicken in marinade 45 minutes or until tender, turning halfway through cooking. Serve with hot cooked noodles and Zucchini and Peppers (p. 160).

CHICKEN PATTIES
▼▼▼

½	large chicken breast (about 6 oz., bone in)
¼ cup	quick-cooking rolled oats
3 tbsp.	milk
¼ tsp.	salt
1 tsp.	melted butter
	Dash pepper
	Dash ground nutmeg
¼ cup	fine dry bread crumbs
1	egg, lightly beaten
1 tbsp.	margarine or olive oil
	Mushroom Sauce (p. 258)

Preparation:
15 minutes
Cooking:
10 minutes

Skin and bone chicken breast and put it through the food chopper or whirl it in food processor (see note). Combine rolled oats and milk and let stand 5 minutes.

Combine ground chicken (you should have ½ to ¾ cup) and rolled oats and add salt, butter, pepper, and nutmeg. The mixture will be quite soft.

Drop half the mixture into the bread crumbs and roll it around to pick up some of the crumbs, then shape into a thick patty. Repeat with second half of mixture, then dip each into egg and back into bread crumbs to coat well. Chill.

Heat margarine or oil in small skillet and cook the patties over medium heat until well browned and cooked through, about 5 minutes a side. Serve with Mushroom Sauce and add hot buttered noodles and broiled tomato.

Note: Many places sell ground raw chicken. If you are buying it already ground, you will need about ¼ lb. for this recipe.

GENERAL RULES
FOR MICROWAVING CHICKEN

▼ Allow 6 to 8 minutes at high per pound of chicken in 600 to 700 watt oven.

▼ Completely thaw chicken before microwaving.

▼ Standing time is important. Cooking will be completed during this time. Allow at least 5 minutes of standing time. Test doneness of chicken after standing time.

▼ Cover chicken in microwave to be sure of complete, even cooking and to avoid splatters.

▼ Do not salt chicken before cooking in microwave.

ITALIAN OVEN-FRIED WINGS
▼▼▼

6	chicken wings
1½ tbsp.	olive oil
½	small clove garlic
3 tbsp.	flour
1 tbsp.	grated Parmesan cheese
	Pinch dried leaf thyme
	Pinch dried leaf oregano
	Dash each salt and pepper

Preparation:
15 minutes
Cooking:
45 minutes

Prepare wings by breaking them at the joints and cutting them apart with a sharp knife. Use the meaty section that was closest to the body and the tasty lower wing piece but put the wing tips in a bag in the freezer to use for soup stock. You will have 12 nice meaty little wing pieces.

Heat oven to 400 °F. Butter a small baking dish, about 8 x 6 x 2 inches. Heat oil and garlic in a small saucepan over low heat 5 minutes. Remove from heat and discard garlic.

Combine flour, cheese, thyme, oregano, salt, and pepper in a plastic bag. Shake wing pieces a few at a time in the mixture, then roll in garlic oil, then shake in flour mixture again. Put close together in prepared baking pan and bake 30 minutes. Turn and continue baking 15 minutes more or until brown and tender. Serve with Mushroom Pilaf (p. 167) and a green salad.

HONEY-GARLIC WINGS
▼▼▼

6	chicken wings, separated (see Italian Oven-Fried Wings p. 66)
2 tbsp.	liquid honey
1 tbsp.	lemon juice
2 tbsp.	water
2 tsp.	ketchup
½	small clove garlic, crushed
¼ tsp.	salt
¼ tsp.	ground ginger
1 tbsp.	butter or margarine

Preparation:
15 minutes
Cooking:
45 minutes
Marinating:
several hours

Heat honey, lemon juice, water, ketchup, garlic, salt, and ginger just to boiling. Pour into a small shallow baking pan, about 8 x 6 x 2 inches. Add separated wings and turn them over in the mixture. Let stand several hours, turning as often as possible.

Heat oven to 400 °F. Lift chicken out of marinade, shaking to remove excess liquid. Pour marinade into a small saucepan, then put butter or margarine in drained pan and set in oven to melt. Put wing pieces in the pan, turning them over in the butter or margarine. Bake 25 minutes, turn pieces and bake 20 minutes more or until tender. Heat marinade and use as a dip. Try eating these as a first course, followed by a large salad.

67

CALIFORNIA CHICKEN ALMOND
▼▼▼

1 tbsp.	butter or margarine
½ cup	sliced mushrooms
2 tsp.	flour
1 cup	chicken stock (p. 126)
	Dash each salt and pepper
	Pinch dried leaf marjoram
	Pinch dried leaf savory
½ cup	cooked rice (p. 168)
1 cup	cut-up cooked chicken
1 tbsp.	chopped pimento
1 tbsp.	chopped parsley
¼ cup	slivered toasted almonds
¼ cup	fine dry bread crumbs
1 tsp.	butter or margarine, melted

Preparation:
15 minutes
Cooking:
30 minutes

Heat oven to 375 °F. Butter a small casserole, about 2 cup size.

Heat 1 tbsp. butter or margarine in a medium saucepan. Add mushrooms and stir over medium heat 2 minutes. Sprinkle in flour and stir to blend.

Remove from heat and add chicken stock, salt, pepper, marjoram, and savory. Stir to blend and return to heat. Stir until boiling, thickened, and smooth. Reduce heat and simmer 3 minutes.

Add rice, chicken, pimento, parsley, and half the almonds to the sauce, then turn mixture into the prepared casserole.

Combine bread crumbs, 1 tsp. melted butter or margarine, and remaining almonds and sprinkle over all. Bake about 30 minutes or until bubbling well.

Note: Use 1 cup water and ½ tsp. chicken stock mix in place of stock if desired.

CREAMED CHICKEN ON TOAST
▼▼▼

1 tbsp.	butter or margarine
¼ cup	fresh mushrooms, sliced
¼ cup	slivered green pepper
1 tbsp.	flour
¼ tsp.	salt
	Dash pepper
½ cup	chicken stock (p. 126)
¼ cup	light cream
1	egg yolk, lightly beaten
1 cup	cut-up cooked chicken
1 tbsp.	chopped pimento
1 tbsp.	dry sherry (optional)
	Buttered whole wheat toast or English muffin

Preparation:
10 minutes
Cooking:
10 minutes

Heat butter or margarine in medium saucepan. Add mushrooms and green pepper and stir over medium heat 3 minutes. Sprinkle in flour, salt, and pepper and stir to blend. Remove from heat and stir in chicken stock and cream. Return to heat and stir until boiling, thickened, and smooth. Gradually stir about half the sauce into the egg yolk, then return the mixture to the saucepan and bring just to a boil.

Add chicken, pimento, and sherry and heat well. Serve on toast or English muffin.

Note: Use ½ cup water and ¼ tsp. chicken stock mix in place of stock if desired.

GLAZED CORNISH HEN
▼▼▼

⅔ cup	water
¼ cup	long grain rice
2 tbsp.	coarsely chopped pecans
1 tbsp.	olive oil
4	medium mushrooms, sliced
1	small onion, sliced
½	small clove garlic, minced
3 tbsp.	orange juice
1 tbsp.	white wine
1 tsp.	grated orange rind
¼ tsp.	salt
	Dash pepper
1	small piece bay leaf, crumbled
	Pinch dried leaf marjoram
	Pinch dried leaf savory
	Pinch ground nutmeg
1	Cornish hen (thawed if frozen)
	Salt and pepper
2 tsp.	butter or margarine
2 tsp.	olive oil

Preparation:
30 minutes
Cooking:
1 hour

Bring water to a boil in a small saucepan. Add rice and stir with a fork, then reduce heat to low, cover tightly, and cook 20 minutes. Check and if water still remains, simmer for a few minutes with lid off.

71

Heat oven to 350 °F. Toast pecans lightly in oven. Grease a small baking dish, about 8 x 6 x 2 inches.

Heat 1 tbsp. oil in small heavy skillet over high heat. Add mushrooms, onion, and garlic and stir 2 minutes. Add mushroom mixture and pecans to cooked rice and toss lightly with a fork. Spread in prepared baking pan.

Combine orange juice, wine, orange rind, salt, pepper, bay leaf, marjoram, savory, and nutmeg in a small saucepan and simmer 10 minutes. Set aside. Sprinkle inside of hen lightly with salt and pepper. Fold wings under back and tie legs close to body, tucking tail into cavity.

Heat butter or margarine and 2 tsp. oil in skillet used for mushroom mixture and brown bird lightly on all sides over medium heat. Set bird on top of rice and brush with orange juice mixture.

Cover pan with foil and roast 50 minutes, uncovering and brushing with orange juice mixture several times. (If orange juice mixture thickens or dries up add a little more wine.) Increase oven temperature to 400 °F. Brush bird with juice mixture and cook uncovered until tender and golden, about 10 minutes more.

TURKEY WITH ORANGE GRAVY
▼▼▼

½	turkey breast (about 1 lb. 4 oz.)
	Cooking oil
¾ cup	orange juice
6 tbsp.	dry white wine
1 tbsp.	flour
¼ cup	water
1 tsp.	grated orange rind
1 tsp.	sugar
	Salt and pepper

Preparation:
5 minutes
Cooking:
2 hours

Heat oven to 325°F. Put turkey breast on rack in small roasting pan. Brush with oil. Add ½ cup of the orange juice and ¼ cup of the wine to the pan. Cover pan loosely with foil and roast about 1¾ hours, basting with pan juices occasionally and uncovering for the last 15 minutes. (A meat thermometer will register 180°F.)

Put turkey on a hot platter and pour drippings in roasting pan into a measuring cup or small deep bowl. Chill by adding ice cubes until fat rises. Discard fat. Return remaining liquid to the roasting pan along with the remaining ¼ cup orange juice and 2 tbsp. wine. Heat, stirring up any browned bits from the bottom of the pan. Shake flour and water together until smooth and stir into boiling liquid gradually. Stir in orange rind and sugar. Taste and season with salt and pepper. Thin with a little more wine if necessary. Reduce heat and simmer 5 minutes. Slice turkey and serve with gravy. Sweet Potato with Maple Syrup (p. 157) and steamed broccoli or any other green vegetable are good with this.

Leftover roast turkey can be used in place of chicken in California Chicken Almond (p. 68) or Creamed Chicken on Toast (p. 70) or in salads (pp. 172, 186, 187, and 188).

FOUR-WAY TURKEY BREAST

2½ lb.   **fresh turkey breast cut into 2 sides and prepared this way:**

▼ One side left with bone in for Turkey with Orange Gravy (p. 73)

▼ Second side boned and prepared this way:

1. Cut 2 thick slices (½-inch) across the breast (just as if you are carving), flatten and use as directed in Turkey Cutlets (p. 75).

2. Cut remaining turkey meat in half and slice 1 piece in thin strips across the grain to use for Turkey Stir-Fry (p. 77).

3. Grind remaining turkey meat through meat chopper or in food processor to use for Turkey Burgers in Garlic Sauce (p. 78).

You must have fresh (not frozen or previously frozen turkey breast) for this since you will want to freeze some of these bits and pieces for the future. You will probably be able to find turkey cutlets, ground turkey, and even turkey strips for stir-fry in turkey specialty shops and in some supermarkets, so if you don't want to prepare your own turkey this way you can still use the recipes.

TURKEY CUTLETS
▼▼▼

1 or 2	raw turkey slices, cut ½ inch thick (see Four-Way Turkey Breast p. 74)
1	egg
1 tsp.	milk
¼ cup	fairly coarse soda cracker crumbs
1 tbsp.	butter or margarine
1 tbsp.	lemon juice
¼ tsp.	dried leaf tarragon
¼ cup	water
¼ tsp.	chicken stock mix
	Dash each salt and pepper
2	thin slices lemon
½ tsp.	cornstarch
2 tbsp.	water

> **Preparation:**
> 5 minutes
> **Cooking:**
> 22 minutes

Put turkey slice(s) between two sheets of waxed paper and pound with a rolling pin or mallet until about ⅛ inch thick.

Beat egg and milk in a flat plate. Put soda cracker crumbs on waxed paper. Dip turkey slice(s) into egg, then into crumbs to coat well on both sides. Heat butter or margarine in a medium skillet over medium heat. Add turkey and cook until lightly browned on both sides. Lift out and set aside. Reduce heat to low, add lemon juice to drippings in pan, then add tarragon, ¼ cup water, and stock mix. Return turkey to pan, sprinkle lightly with salt and pepper, and top with lemon slices. Cover and simmer about 15 minutes or until fork-tender.

Put turkey on a hot plate. Bring liquid in skillet to a boil. Mix cornstarch and 2 tbsp. water and stir enough of mixture into boiling liquid to thicken slightly. Boil 1 minute, then pour over turkey.

TURKEY STIR-FRY
▼▼▼

1 tbsp.	cooking oil
½ cup	thin strips raw turkey (see Four-Way Turkey Breast p. 74)
1	small onion, sliced
1	small clove garlic, minced
½ tsp.	minced fresh ginger
¼ cup	small squares green pepper
½ cup	thin sliced broccoli
¼ cup	thin sliced celery
1 tbsp.	water
1 tsp.	cornstarch
1 tsp.	soya sauce
⅓ cup	water
6	cashews or toasted almonds

Preparation:
10 minutes
Cooking:
about 5 minutes

Heat oil in large heavy skillet or wok. Add strips of turkey and fry until all pink disappears. Lift out turkey and set aside.

Add onion, garlic, and ginger to pan and stir briskly over high heat 1 minute. Add green pepper, broccoli, and celery and stir 1 minute. Add 1 tbsp. water, cover tightly, and steam 1 minute. Return turkey to pan and heat.

Combine cornstarch, soya sauce, and ⅓ cup water and stir into liquid in pan. Boil until slightly thickened and clear. Serve immediately with hot cooked rice and garnish with nuts.

TURKEY BURGERS IN GARLIC SAUCE
▼▼▼

1 cup (approx.)	**ground raw turkey (See Four-Way Turkey Breast p. 74)**
½ cup	**soft bread crumbs**
1 tbsp.	**chopped onion**
¼ tsp.	**salt**
	Dash pepper
¼ tsp.	**poultry seasoning**
1	**egg, lightly beaten**
	Flour
1 tbsp.	**cooking oil**
⅓ cup	**ketchup**
1 tbsp.	**white vinegar**
1 tbsp.	**brown sugar**
¼ tsp.	**ground ginger**
2 tsp.	**soya sauce**
1	**large clove garlic, crushed**
1 tsp.	**cornstarch**

> Preparation:
> 10 minutes
> Cooking:
> 20 to 25 minutes

Combine first seven ingredients, blending well with a fork. Mixture will be soft. Put a small amount of flour on waxed paper. Shape turkey mixture into two thick cakes with hands rinsed under cold water. Dip the cakes into flour to coat both sides. Heat oil in medium skillet over medium heat and brown cakes well on both sides.

Combine remaining ingredients and pour over. Cover and simmer 15 minutes, turning cakes once. Serve with rice and Peas French Style (p. 147).

OVEN-BARBECUED TURKEY LEG
▼▼▼

1	turkey leg, about 1 lb.
1 tbsp.	flour
	Dash each salt and pepper
¼ tsp.	paprika
1 tbsp.	butter or margarine
1 tbsp.	cooking oil
1	small onion, chopped
1	small clove garlic, minced
1 tbsp.	lemon juice
1 tbsp.	Worcestershire sauce
	Dash Tabasco sauce
½ cup	water
¼ cup	ketchup
	Dash each salt and pepper
1 tsp.	sugar
½ tsp.	chili powder
	Pinch dried leaf oregano

> **Preparation:**
> 30 minutes
> **Cooking:**
> 1 hour, 10 minutes

Separate leg into thigh and drumstick. Heat oven to 375 °F. Combine flour, salt, pepper, and paprika and roll turkey pieces in mixture. Heat butter or margarine and oil in skillet, brown turkey pieces slowly, then put in a small baking dish. Add onion and garlic to skillet and stir over medium heat 2 minutes. Add all remaining ingredients, bring to a boil, reduce heat, and simmer 10 minutes. Pour over turkey pieces, cover, and bake 30 minutes. Turn turkey pieces, cover, and bake 30 minutes. Uncover and bake until tender, about 10 minutes. Baste often.

79

CHINESE-STYLE FISH
▼▼▼

1	fillet cod (or other white fish), ¼ to ⅓ lb.
½ lb.	fresh asparagus
1 tbsp.	cooking oil
	Dash salt
1½ tbsp.	cooking oil
	Grating fresh pepper
¼ cup	water
½ tsp.	soya sauce
1 tsp.	cornstarch

Preparation:
10 minutes
Cooking:
6 minutes

Cut fish into pieces about 2 x 1 inch. Wash and trim asparagus and cut on the diagonal into 1-inch pieces. Dip pieces into cold water, drain immediately but do not dry.

Heat 1 tbsp. oil in heavy skillet over high heat (use a wok if you have one). Add wet asparagus, sprinkle with salt, and stir constantly until tender-crisp but still bright green, about 3 minutes. Lift out with slotted spoon onto a hot platter and keep hot.

Add 1½ tbsp. oil to skillet and drop in the fish pieces. Sprinkle lightly with pepper. Stir constantly over high heat until fish flakes easily with a fork, about 2 minutes. Lift out with slotted spoon and put on the platter with the asparagus.

Combine water, soya sauce, and cornstarch, add to any liquid remaining in pan, and stir until thick and clear. Pour over fish. Buttered Celery and Onion (p. 143) and rice are nice with this dish.

ISLAND COD
▼▼▼

1	fillet cod
1 tbsp.	lime juice
1 tbsp.	water
2 tsp.	chopped onion
¼ tsp.	salt
	Dash pepper
¼ tsp.	ground ginger
¼ tsp.	grated lime rind
	Small piece bay leaf, crumbled
2	lime slices

Preparation:
5 minutes
Cooking:
15 minutes
Microwave:
3 minutes

Oil a baking dish just large enough to hold the fish. Put fish in baking dish. Combine all remaining ingredients except lime slices and pour over. Cover and let stand in the refrigerator 1 hour, turning once.

Heat oven to 350 °F. Top fish with lime slices, cover, and bake 10 minutes, then uncover and bake about 5 minutes longer until fish flakes easily with a fork.

To microwave: Put fish in a baking dish that will just hold it. Add the marinade as suggested above, cover with transparent wrap, and let stand in refrigerator 1 hour, turning once. Cut 2 slits in the transparent wrap with the tip of a sharp knife and microwave at high 1 minute. Uncover, spoon pan juices over fish, top with lime slices, cover again, and microwave 2 minutes. Let stand, covered, 3 minutes.

Cucumber Salad (p. 174) is a nice accompaniment to this dish.

81

GENERAL RULES
FOR MICROWAVING FISH

Since fish is naturally tender, it needs minimum cooking. (If fish is frozen, thaw completely before cooking.) If the outside is opaque and the center not quite done, it's fine. The center will finish cooking while the fish stands for a short time. For 1 or 2 fillets or steaks about ½ inch thick, you should need only 3 or 4 minutes at high power. Put steaks on paper towel in baking dish, brush with melted butter or margarine, sprinkle with lemon juice and dill if desired, and cover loosely with waxed paper. Microwave minimum time, then check to see if fish flakes easily.

Or, for whole, small fish, such as trout, brush fish with melted butter or margarine in baking dish. If you are leaving the head and tail on, it is all right to wrap them with foil. Cover the baking dish tightly with transparent wrap and turn back one corner to vent. Microwave on high. A small trout weighing about ½ lb. takes only 3 to 4 minutes.

BAKED FISH SCANDINAVIAN STYLE

¼ cup	buttermilk
	Small piece bay leaf, crumbled
1	peppercorn, coarsely crushed
1	whole clove, coarsely crushed
½ tsp.	grated onion
⅓ to ½ lb.	fresh or frozen cod
	Pepper
	Garlic salt
¼ tsp.	dried dill weed
	Paprika

Preparation: 5 minutes
Cooking: 10 to 15 minutes

Heat oven to 375°F. Lightly oil a shallow baking dish just large enough to hold the fish.

Combine buttermilk, bay leaf, peppercorn, clove, and onion. Put fish in baking dish, sprinkle lightly with pepper, garlic salt, and dill weed, pour buttermilk mixture over, and sprinkle with paprika.

Bake about 10 minutes for fresh fish and 15 minutes for frozen or until the fish flakes easily with a fork.

BROILED FISH

1	slice bacon, finely chopped
1	fresh cod, sole, or haddock fillet
	Salt and pepper
	Chili powder
½ tsp.	lemon juice
½	small tomato, peeled, seeded, and finely chopped
1	green onion, finely chopped

Preparation:
10 minutes
Cooking:
4 to 5 minutes

Cook bacon bits in a small skillet over medium heat until transparent but not crisp. Drain well on paper towelling.

Cover the rack of a broiler pan with aluminum foil. Oil lightly and lay fish on it. Sprinkle fish lightly with salt, pepper, and chili powder and drizzle with lemon juice. Turn oven to broil.

Combine tomato, green onion, and bacon bits and spoon over the fish. Slip close under hot broiler and broil 4 to 5 minutes or until fish flakes easily with a fork. It won't be necessary to turn the fish if the fillet is thin. Creamy Noodles (p. 163) make a tasty addition along with a green salad.

CURRIED FILLET OF HADDOCK
▼▼▼

1	slice day-old white bread
1½ tbsp.	mayonnaise
½ tsp.	curry powder
	Salt and pepper
1	fillet haddock, about ½ inch thick
1 tbsp.	commercial chutney (see note)
2 tsp.	lime juice
	Lime wedge

Preparation:
7 minutes
Cooking:
10 to 15 minutes

Heat oven to 400 °F. Cut crusts from bread and break bread into very small pieces or break up coarsely in food processor. Spread on a baking sheet and heat in oven to dry slightly but not brown.

Combine mayonnaise, curry powder, and a light sprinkling of salt and pepper. Spread one side of fish with half the mayonnaise mixture, then turn that side down into the crumbs. Spread second side with mayonnaise mixture and coat with remaining crumbs. Lightly oil a shallow baking pan just large enough to hold the fish and put fish in it. Bake about 15 minutes, turning carefully after 5 minutes. If fish is thinner than ½ inch, check after 10 minutes. Cook only until it flakes easily with a fork. Combine chutney and lime juice and serve with fish. Garnish with lime wedge.

Note: Some commercial chutney has large pieces of fruit. If yours has, either use just the liquid part, or chop the fruit very finely. This chutney mixture livens up any plain fish dish.

EASY SWEET-SOUR STEAMED FISH
▼▼▼

1 fillet	sole, 3 to 4 oz.
1 tbsp.	sugar
1 tbsp.	lemon juice
1 tsp.	slivered candied or preserved ginger
2 tsp.	toasted slivered almonds

Preparation:
5 minutes
Cooking:
Steam 6 minutes
Microwave:
5 minutes

Set the fish fillet on lightly oiled heavy foil, turning the edges of the foil up enough to form a "dish" around the fish. Set in a skillet of simmering water, cover tightly, and steam about 6 minutes or until fish flakes easily with a fork.

Heat sugar and lemon juice just until sugar is dissolved. Put fish on hot serving plate, pour lemon mixture over, and garnish with ginger and almonds.

To microwave: Put fish in a shallow dish (a glass pie pan works fine) and cover the pan with damp paper towel. Microwave 2 minutes at high and let stand, covered, 3 minutes.

Put sugar and lemon juice in a small dish and heat at high 30 seconds or just until sugar is dissolved. Complete dish as above.

Asparagus Chinese Style (p. 133) is a nice addition.

BAKED FISH CREOLE
▼▼▼

1	fillet sole, about 3 oz.
1 tsp.	thinly sliced green onion
1 tsp.	finely chopped green pepper
1	medium mushroom, finely chopped
⅓ cup	canned tomatoes (see note)
½ tsp.	lemon juice
	Pinch sugar
⅛ tsp.	dry mustard
	Pinch dried leaf oregano
	Dash each salt and pepper

Preparation:
10 minutes
Cooking:
10 minutes
Microwave:
5 minutes

Heat oven to 450 °F. Cut fish (it doesn't have to be thawed if frozen) into 1-inch squares and put in a small casserole, about 2 cup size. Combine remaining ingredients in a small saucepan and simmer 5 minutes. Pour over fish and bake about 10 minutes or until fish flakes easily.

To microwave: Thaw fish if frozen and cut into 1-inch squares. Combine all remaining ingredients in a 1-qt. casserole. Cover and microwave at high 3 minutes, stirring after each minute. Add fish pieces, stir, cover with damp paper towel and microwave at high 2 minutes, stirring after 1 minute. Let stand, covered, 3 minutes.

Note: To measure the tomatoes, cut up 1 good-size piece of tomato into measuring cup, then add enough juice to make the ⅓ cup.

BAKED HALIBUT
▼▼▼

1	small halibut steak or a piece of a steak, ½ inch thick (about 5 or 6 oz.)
	Salt, paprika, and cayenne
2 tsp.	lemon juice
½ tsp.	cooking oil
2 tbsp.	chopped onion
2	strips green pepper, about 2 inches long by ¼ inch wide

Preparation:
incl. standing time
1 hour, 5 minutes
Cooking:
10 minutes
Microwave:
4 minutes

Put halibut in a small baking dish. Sprinkle lightly with salt, paprika, and cayenne and drizzle with lemon juice. Cover and let stand in the refrigerator at least 1 hour, turning once. Heat oven to 450 °F. Heat oil in a small skillet and fry onion over medium heat 2 minutes. Spread over fish. Add green pepper strips and bake about 10 minutes or until fish flakes easily, basting with pan liquid once or twice.

To microwave: Put fish in small baking dish, prepare as described above, cover with transparent wrap, and marinate in refrigerator 1 hour.

Put oil in a small dish or glass measuring cup. Add onion, stir, and microwave at high 1 minute. Spread over fish and add green pepper strips. Cover again and cut 2 slits in transparent wrap with the tip of a sharp knife. Microwave at high 3 minutes, rotating dish ½ turn after 2 minutes, or until small ends of fish flake easily but center is still translucent. Let stand, covered, 3 minutes.

POACHED TROUT
▼▼▼

½ cup	dry white wine
½ cup	water
1	small carrot, thinly sliced
1	slice onion
1	small bunch celery leaves
	Sprig parsley
2	peppercorns
1	small trout (7 or 8 inches)

Preparation:
5 minutes
Cooking:
9 minutes
Microwave:
6 minutes

Combine all ingredients except trout in a skillet large enough to hold the fish, bring to a boil, reduce heat, and simmer 5 minutes. Add fish, adding enough water to just cover it, and simmer about 4 minutes or until fish flakes easily. Remove from liquid immediately.

To microwave: Put all ingredients except the fish in a baking dish that will just hold the trout. Cover and put in microwave at high just until mixture comes to a boil, about 3 minutes. Add fish, cover with transparent wrap, slit the wrap in 2 places with the tip of a sharp knife and microwave at high about 3 minutes, turning the fish and rotating the dish once. Let stand covered, 5 minutes.

If you wish, chill this fish and serve on a salad plate with a sauce made by combining ¼ cup plain yogurt, 1 tsp. lemon juice, pinch salt, and ¼ tsp. snipped fresh dill.

COLD SALMON
▼▼▼

1	small salmon steak, ¾ inch thick (about 4 oz.)
	Pepper
1 tsp.	soft butter or margarine
1	paper-thin onion slice
1 tbsp.	white wine
1	large sprig dill

Preparation:
3 minutes
Cooking:
20 minutes
Microwave:
3 minutes

Heat oven to 400°F. Put salmon on a piece of foil large enough to wrap it completely. Add remaining ingredients and fold the foil so it is airtight. Put it in a small baking dish and bake about 20 minutes. Chill.

To microwave: Put salmon in a small baking dish just large enough to hold it and add remaining ingredients. Cover with transparent wrap and cut 2 slits in wrap with the tip of a sharp knife. Microwave at high 3 minutes or until small ends of fish flake easily but center is still translucent. Turn dish after 1 minute and baste fish with liquid in pan. Cover again and continue cooking. Let stand, covered, 5 minutes, then chill.

For a special summer meal, serve with potato salad or boiled new potatoes and tiny new carrots.

Note: If you have no fresh dill, sprinkle about ¼ tsp. dried dill weed over salmon.

TUNA ON ENGLISH MUFFIN

1 tbsp.	butter or margarine
1	green onion, sliced paper thin
¼ cup	chopped celery
2 tsp.	flour
1	can (3.75 oz. or 106 g) tuna, drained and flaked
¼ cup	cubed process cheese
¼ cup	milk
1 tbsp.	finely chopped dill pickle
2 tbsp.	sour cream or plain yogurt
½ tsp.	lemon juice
¼ tsp.	snipped fresh dill
	Grating fresh pepper
1	English muffin, split, toasted, and buttered

Preparation:
15 minutes
Cooking:
7 minutes

Melt butter or margarine in small saucepan over low heat. Add onion and celery and stir over medium heat 2 minutes. Sprinkle in flour and stir to blend. Remove from heat and stir in tuna, cheese, milk, and dill pickle. Return to medium heat and simmer, stirring, 3 minutes. Stir in sour cream or yogurt, lemon juice, snipped dill, and pepper and heat but do not boil. Serve over English muffin.

91

SHRIMP AND GREEN BEANS
▼▼▼

¼ lb.	raw shrimp
1 tsp.	cooking oil
1 tbsp.	thinly sliced green onions
½	small clove garlic, crushed
¼ tsp.	finely chopped fresh ginger
¼ cup	chicken stock (p. 126)
	Dash each salt and pepper
1 cup	frozen cut green beans (not frenched)
¼ tsp.	cornstarch
1 tsp.	cold water

Preparation:
10 minutes
Cooking:
10 minutes

Shell and clean shrimp. Heat 1 tsp. oil in small heavy skillet, add onions, garlic, and ginger. Cook gently 1 minute, stirring. Add shrimp and half the chicken stock and cook gently, stirring, until shrimp has turned bright pink, about 3 minutes. Lift out shrimp.

Add remaining stock, salt, pepper, and beans, cover and simmer 5 minutes or until beans are just tender. Return shrimp to pan and heat. Stir cornstarch and water together and stir into liquid in pan. Cook until thick and clear.

Corn-Stuffed Tomato (p. 158) contrasts nicely with this dish.

Note: Use ¼ cup water and ⅛ tsp. chicken stock mix in place of stock if desired.

SHRIMP AND CUCUMBER
▼▼▼

¼ lb.	raw shrimp
1 tsp.	dry sherry
	Pinch salt
¼ tsp.	sugar
¼ tsp.	cornstarch
½	medium cucumber
2 tsp.	cooking oil
1 tsp.	cooking oil
¼ cup	sliced fresh mushrooms
1	green onion, sliced paper thin

Preparation: 10 minutes
Cooking: 5 minutes

Shell and clean shrimp. Put them in a bowl. Combine sherry, salt, sugar, and cornstarch and add to shrimp, stirring to coat shrimp with mixture as much as possible.

Peel cucumber, cut in quarters lengthwise, and scrape out and discard seeds. Cut cucumber into pieces about 1½ inches long.

In heavy skillet or wok, heat 2 tsp. oil until it is very hot. Add shrimp and cook quickly 2 to 3 minutes or until shrimp are bright pink. Lift out with a slotted spoon and keep hot.

Add 1 tsp. oil to pan and add mushrooms and cook quickly 30 seconds. Add cucumber and cook and stir over high heat 2 minutes. Return shrimp to pan and heat 30 seconds, stirring. Serve sprinkled with green onion and add hot cooked rice.

CURRIED CRAB CAKES
▼▼▼

2 tsp.	butter or margarine
1 tbsp.	finely chopped onion
1 tbsp.	finely chopped green pepper
¼ tsp.	curry powder
½ cup	soft bread crumbs
½	can (4.5 oz. or 128 g size) crab
	Dash each salt and pepper
1 tbsp.	chopped parsley
1	egg
1 tsp.	milk
1	hard-cooked egg, finely chopped (p. 105)
	Fine dry bread crumbs
2 tsp.	butter or margarine
	Chutney

Preparation:
15 minutes
Cooking:
13 minutes

Melt 2 tsp. butter or margarine in a small skillet. Add onion, green pepper, and curry powder and cook gently, stirring 3 minutes.

Put soft bread crumbs in a bowl. Drain crab and break up finely (you should have about ½ cup). Add to bread crumbs along with salt and pepper, parsley, and curry mixture. Beat egg and milk together lightly with a fork and add to mixture, blend well with the fork, then add the hard-cooked egg and blend again.

Shape mixture into 2 thick cakes. Dip them into fine dry bread crumbs to coat both sides. Heat 2 tsp. butter or margarine in skillet used earlier, add crab cakes, and fry over medium heat until well browned on the outside and heated through. Serve hot with chutney and Green Bean Salad (p. 175).

CREAMY CRAB
▼▼▼

½	can (4.5 oz. or 128 g size) crab
1 tbsp.	butter or margarine
½ cup	sliced fresh mushrooms
1 tbsp.	flour
⅓ cup	light cream
2 tbsp.	dry white wine
2 tsp.	lemon juice
¼ tsp.	dried dill weed
1 tbsp.	chopped pimento
	Salt and pepper
1 tbsp.	grated Parmesan cheese
	Chopped parsley
	Hot cooked rice

Preparation:
10 minutes
Cooking:
5 to 7 minutes

Drain and break up crab, setting aside 1 or 2 large pieces for garnish.

Heat butter or margarine in a small saucepan. Add mushrooms and stir over medium heat 2 minutes. Sprinkle in flour and stir to blend. Remove from heat and stir in cream and wine (don't worry if mixture appears to curdle — it will be smooth when cooked). Return to heat and stir until boiling, thickened, and smooth. Stir in lemon juice, dill weed, pimento, and crab. Taste and add salt and pepper if needed.

At this point you can do any of the following:

▼ Serve over rice sprinkled with a mixture of Parmesan cheese and parsley. Garnish with large pieces of crab you set aside.

▼ Turn mixture into an individual serving dish, sprinkle with Parmesan cheese and parsley, and slip under hot broiler to brown lightly. Garnish with large pieces of crab you set aside.

▼ As a nice starter for a special meal for two, spoon mixture into two buttered scallop shells, sprinkle with Parmesan cheese and parsley, and brown under the broiler. Garnish with pieces of crab you set aside.

BAKED SCALLOPS

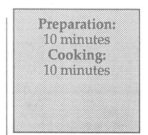

¼ lb.	scallops, fresh or frozen
½ tsp.	lemon juice
1 tsp.	butter or margarine
2 tbsp.	dry white wine
2	medium mushrooms, thinly sliced
2 tbsp.	Crème Fraîche (p. 255) or plain yogurt
2 tsp.	fine dry bread crumbs
1 slice	bacon, optional

Preparation:
10 minutes
Cooking:
10 minutes

Thaw scallops if using frozen. Butter a scallop shell or small baking dish and add the scallops (cut very large ones in half). Drizzle with lemon juice. Melt butter or margarine in a small skillet over high heat. Remove from heat and add wine. Return to heat and cook quickly until wine is nearly cooked away, 2 to 3 minutes, then add mushrooms and stir 2 minutes. Remove from heat and stir in Crème Fraîche or yogurt. Spoon over scallops and sprinkle with crumbs.

Heat oven to 400 °F at serving time. Fry bacon just until cooked but not crisp. Drain on paper towel, then shape into a small loose roll and set on top of scallops. Bake until scallops are cooked, about 10 minutes. Rice Salad (p. 182) makes an unusual combination.

SCALLOPS IN SAUCE
▼▼▼

¼ lb.	scallops, fresh or frozen
1	slice bacon, cut in small pieces
1 tsp.	minced green onion
1½ tbsp.	chili sauce
1 tbsp.	white wine
½ tsp.	Worcestershire sauce
	Dash Tabasco sauce
	Dash each salt and pepper

Preparation: 5 minutes
Cooking: 10 minutes
Microwave: 3½ minutes

Thaw scallops if using frozen and cut any very large ones in half. Cook bacon bits in a small saucepan until limp, add onion, and stir over medium heat 3 minutes or until bacon has browned lightly. Stir in remaining ingredients including scallops and simmer until scallops are tender, about 5 minutes. Stir occasionally.

To microwave: Thaw scallops if using frozen and cut any very large ones in half. Put bacon bits in a small casserole, about 2 cup size. Cover with waxed paper and microwave at high 1 minute. Add onion and microwave at high 1 minute, stirring after 30 seconds. Add remaining ingredients and scallops, stir, cover with transparent wrap, cut 2 slits in the wrap with the tip of a sharp knife, and microwave at high 1½ minutes, stirring once. Let stand 3 minutes.

Serve over rice and add a crisp green vegetable such as broccoli or snow peas.

NUT LOAF (Vegetarian main dish)
▼▼▼

2 tsp.	cooking oil
1 tbsp.	chopped onion
⅓ cup	chopped celery
¼ cup	blanched almonds, chopped
¼ cup	walnuts, chopped
½ cup	cooked brown rice
½ cup	1% cottage cheese
1	green onion, chopped
1 tbsp.	toasted wheat germ
1 tbsp.	chopped parsley
	Pinch each dried leaf thyme and dried dill weed
	Grating fresh pepper
1	egg, beaten
1 tbsp.	toasted wheat germ
	Tomato Sauce (p. 259)

Preparation:
12 minutes
Cooking:
30 minutes

Heat oven to 375°F. Grease a small foil loaf pan, about 5½ x 3¼ x 2 inches. Heat oil in a small skillet and add onion. Cook gently 3 minutes. Add celery and stir over medium-low heat 5 minutes.

Put all remaining ingredients except 1 tbsp. wheat germ and Tomato Sauce in a bowl and add onion mixture. Sprinkle the 1 tbsp. wheat germ in the prepared pan and shake it around to coat the bottom of the pan. Turn the nut mixture into the pan and bake 30 minutes or until firm. Let stand in pan 5 minutes, then turn out and cut in thick slices to serve. Top with Tomato Sauce. Makes 2 servings.

VEGETARIAN CHILI
▼▼▼

¼ cup	olive oil
1	small eggplant (about ½ lb.), cut in ½-inch cubes
1 tbsp.	flour
1 tbsp.	chili powder
1	small onion, sliced
1	small green pepper, chopped
1	small clove garlic, minced
1 cup	canned tomatoes
1 cup	kidney beans, drained
½ tsp.	dried leaf oregano
¼ tsp.	ground cumin
¼ tsp.	salt
⅔ cup	water

Preparation:
15 minutes
Cooking:
25 minutes

Heat oil in medium saucepan. Add eggplant and stir over medium heat 5 minutes. Remove from heat and sprinkle in flour and chili powder, stirring to blend through the eggplant. Add remaining ingredients and mix lightly. Bring to a boil over medium heat, cover, reduce heat to medium-low, and cook for about 15 minutes, stirring carefully occasionally. Vegetables should be crisp and not breaking up. Serve in a bowl, and sprinkle with more chopped green pepper and onion if desired. Add some hot buttered whole wheat toast.

Makes 2 servings.

VEGETARIAN LASAGNA
▼▼▼

1	tbsp. olive oil
1	small onion, chopped
1	small clove garlic, crushed
1	small eggplant, diced
1	small zucchini, diced
¼ cup	sliced fresh mushrooms
1½ cups	canned tomatoes
½ cup	dry red wine
¼ cup	chopped green pepper
¼ cup	chopped parsley (Italian if possible)
½ tsp.	dried leaf oregano
¼ tsp.	dried leaf basil
	Grating fresh pepper
½ cup	ricotta cheese
1	egg white
2 tbsp.	chopped parsley
	Lasagna noodles (use the kind you don't have to cook ahead)
⅓ cup	grated mozzarella cheese
2 tbsp.	grated Parmesan cheese

Preparation:
25 minutes
Cooking:
30 minutes

Heat oil in large saucepan. Add onion, garlic, eggplant, zucchini, and mushrooms and cook over low heat, stirring often, 10 minutes. Add tomatoes, breaking up the whole ones with a spoon. Stir in wine, green pepper, ¼ cup parsley, oregano, basil, and pepper. Simmer 30 minutes, stirring often. Combine ricotta cheese, egg white, and 2 tbsp. parsley in blender or food processor and blend until smooth and creamy.

Grease 2 small foil loaf pans, about 5½ x 3¼ x 2 inches, and spread a thin layer of tomato mixture in each. Top with lasagna noodles to cover sauce, breaking the noodles to make them fit. Add ¼ of the ricotta mixture by small spoonfuls on top of noodles in each pan, then sprinkle each with ¼ of the mozzarella cheese. Repeat layers, ending with a layer of sauce. Sprinkle each with 1 tbsp. Parmesan cheese.

At this point you can bake one lasagna and freeze the other or wrap them both in foil and freeze until needed. To bake immediately, heat oven to 350°F and bake about 30 minutes or until bubbling well. If frozen, defrost overnight or during the day in the refrigerator and allow a little longer baking time, about 40 minutes.

ALFALFA OMELET
▼▼▼

2	eggs
1 tbsp.	water
¼ tsp.	salt
	Grating fresh pepper
½ cup	alfalfa sprouts
1 tbsp.	chopped parsley
1 tbsp.	butter or margarine

Preparation:
3 minutes
Cooking:
1 minute

Beat eggs, water, salt, and pepper together with a fork just until blended but not foamy. Combine alfalfa sprouts and parsley in a small dish.

Heat an omelet pan or a small heavy skillet over high heat until very hot (when pan is hot enough a drop of water will dance around on the surface). Add butter or margarine and heat until it foams but isn't brown. Tilt pan so butter coats bottom, then add egg mixture.

As soon as eggs start to set (which should be immediately), stir right around the pan with a fork, lifting edges of omelet to let uncooked egg run under the cooked. Move the pan back and forth to keep the omelet sliding freely. Continue until all uncooked egg has run underneath but top is still moist. This will only take about 30 seconds.

To brown lightly, cook 2 seconds without stirring, but continue moving pan back and forth. Quickly top omelet with alfalfa sprouts mixture, fold in half, and slide out onto hot serving plate.

EGG BEURRE NOIR
▼▼▼

2 tsp.	butter
1	egg
1 tbsp.	butter
1 tbsp.	finely chopped parsley
¼ tsp.	white vinegar

Preparation:
3 minutes
Cooking:
5 minutes

Heat 2 tsp. butter in small skillet and fry egg until done the way you like it. Lift egg out onto hot serving plate. Add 1 tbsp. butter and half the parsley to the skillet and cook slowly until butter is golden brown. Stir in vinegar and remaining parsley and pour over egg.

TO HARD COOK EGGS

Cover eggs in a small deep saucepan with cold water, at least 1 inch above the eggs. Set over high heat and bring to a boil, uncovered. Remove from heat, cover, and let stand 20 minutes. Run under cold water several minutes to cool and peel when ready to use. Using this method, you won't get the ugly dark ring around the yolk that appears when eggs are boiled.

EGG AND ONION
▼▼▼

2 tsp.	butter or margarine
1	small onion, sliced paper thin
	Salt and pepper
1	egg
2 tsp.	fine dry bread crumbs
½ tsp.	butter or margarine, melted
1½ tbsp.	grated process cheese

Preparation:
5 minutes
Cooking:
15 minutes

Heat oven to 350 °F. Butter a small individual baking dish or custard cup, 6 oz. size.

Heat 2 tsp. butter or margarine in a small skillet. Add onion and cook gently, stirring, about 5 minutes or until limp and transparent. Spoon into prepared baking dish. Sprinkle lightly with salt and pepper. Break the egg into the dish, then combine bread crumbs and melted butter or margarine and sprinkle over the egg.

Bake 7 minutes, then sprinkle with grated cheese and bake about 3 minutes more or until cheese is soft and bubbly.

EGGS CREOLE
▼▼▼

1 tbsp.	butter or margarine
2 tbsp.	finely chopped onion
2 tbsp.	finely chopped green pepper
½	small clove garlic, minced
1 tbsp.	chopped parsley
¼ tsp.	salt
	Dash pepper
	Pinch dried leaf savory
	Dash paprika
⅔ cup	canned tomatoes
2	hard-cooked eggs (p. 105)
½ cup	hot cooked rice

Preparation:
10 minutes
Cooking:
20 minutes

Heat butter or margarine in small saucepan over medium heat. Add onion, green pepper, and garlic and stir 5 minutes. Add parsley, salt, pepper, savory, paprika, and tomatoes and simmer 5 minutes.

Cut eggs in half lengthwise and put into sauce, cut side up. Cover and simmer 10 minutes or until eggs are very hot. Spoon over rice and add a green vegetable, steamed until just tender-crisp.

107

BROCCOLI FRITTATA
▼▼▼

1	small stalk broccoli
1 tbsp.	olive oil
⅓ cup	sliced onion
1	small clove garlic, minced (optional)
2	eggs
¼ cup	grated old cheddar cheese
⅛ tsp.	ground nutmeg
¼ tsp.	salt
	Dash pepper

Preparation:
10 minutes
Cooking:
22 minutes

Steam broccoli until just beginning to get tender, about 5 minutes. Chop finely. You will have about ½ cup.

Heat oil in medium skillet (a non-stick surface is helpful), add onion and garlic and cook gently until onion is tender, about 5 minutes.

Beat eggs in a bowl, then add cheese, chopped broccoli, nutmeg, salt, and pepper and beat until blended. Pour into skillet, stir once, then cook over medium-low heat about 5 minutes, only lifting the mixture around the edge to let uncooked mixture run underneath.

When set, invert on hot plate and slide back into the skillet, unbrowned side down. Cook gently until cooked through and very lightly browned, about 5 minutes more.

SOUPS
▼▼▼

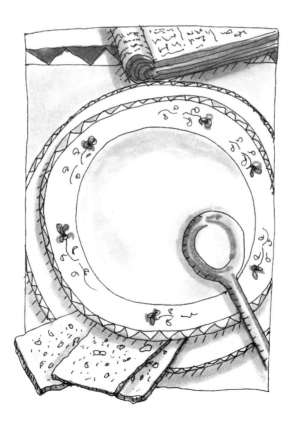

SOUPS
▼▼▼

Soup is the ultimate comfort food. Most of us find we can always manage a bowl with pleasure, no matter how we feel.

If you don't have homemade stock in the refrigerator or freezer, you can still have good soup. In fact, most of these soups are made without stock. They use tomatoes, tomato juice, water, milk, or canned consommé as the base. Of course, I couldn't resist including some soups that need stock, so I have included a recipe for a small amount of chicken stock (p. 126) and another for a larger amount of stock made from meat, chicken, or turkey (p. 127).

Some of these soups are filling enough to make a whole meal with the addition of crusty bread and perhaps a salad. Others are smaller and lighter, just enough to tantalize the taste buds.

BAKED BEAN SOUP
▼▼▼

1 tbsp.	cooking oil
½ cup	match-like strips leftover cooked ham
¼ cup	chopped onion
½	small clove garlic, minced
1 cup	baked beans in tomato sauce
1 cup	canned tomatoes
	Dash each salt and pepper
	Small piece bay leaf, crumbled
	Pinch dried leaf thyme

Preparation:
10 minutes
Cooking:
20 minutes

Heat oil in medium saucepan. Add ham, onion, and garlic and cook gently 3 minutes. Put beans and tomatoes in the blender and blend until smooth. Add to ham mixture and stir in remaining ingredients. Bring to a boil, reduce heat, cover, and simmer gently 15 minutes, stirring often. Thin with a little tomato juice or water if desired.

Makes 1 large or 2 small servings.

WHOLE MEAL SOUP
▼▼▼

1 tbsp.	olive oil
½ lb.	lean ground beef
1	small onion, thinly sliced
½ cup	thinly sliced celery
1 cup	canned tomatoes
1 cup	water
1 cup	canned kidney beans
¼ tsp.	salt
½ tsp.	chili powder
	Dash black pepper
1 cup	thinly sliced cabbage

Preparation:
10 minutes
Cooking:
20 minutes

Heat oil in medium saucepan over medium heat. Add beef and cook until lightly browned and crumbly, breaking apart with a wooden spoon. Add onion and celery and cook gently, stirring 5 minutes. Stir in tomatoes (break up large pieces with wooden spoon), water, beans, salt, chili powder, and pepper and heat to boiling. Reduce heat, cover, and simmer 5 minutes. Add cabbage, cover, and cook until cabbage is tender, about 5 minutes.

Makes 2 big servings.

CABBAGE BREAD SOUP
▼▼▼

2 tbsp.	olive oil
1	small clove garlic
1	slice dry white bread
1	small onion, chopped
1	small tomato, peeled, seeded, and chopped finely
1 tbsp.	diced pimento
1 cup	thinly sliced cabbage
2 cups	water
¼ tsp.	dried leaf basil
1 tbsp.	chopped parsley
¼ tsp.	salt
	Dash pepper

Preparation:
10 minutes
Cooking:
35 minutes

Heat oil in medium saucepan over medium heat. Add garlic and bread and cook, removing garlic when it is golden. Turn the bread slice until dark golden brown on both sides. Drain and cool garlic and bread on paper towelling. Add onion and tomato to saucepan, reduce heat, and stir until onion is tender, about 5 minutes. Stir in pimento and cabbage and cook, stirring over low heat, 5 minutes.

Break bread into small pieces into the blender. Add garlic and about ½ cup of the water. Blend until smooth. Stir remaining water, basil, parsley, salt, and pepper into saucepan and bring to a boil, then stir in the bread mixture. Bring back to a boil, reduce heat, cover, and simmer 20 minutes. Taste and correct seasoning.

Makes 2 servings.

CREAM OF CARROT SOUP
▼▼▼

1 cup	sliced carrots
¼ cup	chopped onion
¼ tsp.	salt
½ cup	boiling water
1½ cups	cold water
¾ cup	skim milk powder
1 tbsp.	soft butter or margarine
1 tbsp.	flour
	Dash pepper
1 tbsp.	chopped parsley

Preparation:
5 minutes
Cooking:
15 minutes

Combine carrots, onion, salt, and boiling water in a medium saucepan. Cover and cook over medium heat until vegetables are tender, about 10 minutes. Turn vegetables and their liquid into a blender and blend until smooth. Add half the cold water, skim milk powder, butter or margarine, flour, and pepper and blend again until smooth. Return to saucepan, add parsley and remaining water, and bring to a boil. Reduce heat and simmer 2 minutes.

Makes 2 servings.

CHEESE AND VEGETABLE CHOWDER
▼▼▼

1 tbsp.	butter or margarine
	Small piece garlic
1 tbsp.	finely chopped onion
1	small carrot, finely grated
2 tbsp.	finely chopped celery
2 tsp.	flour
	Dash each salt and pepper
1 cup	2% or skim milk
¼ cup	grated old cheddar cheese

Preparation:
5 minutes
Cooking:
15 minutes

Melt butter or margarine in small saucepan. Add garlic and cook gently, stirring, 3 minutes. Discard garlic. Add onion, carrot, and celery to pan and stir over low heat until vegetables are tender-crisp, about 5 minutes. Sprinkle in flour, salt, and pepper and stir to blend. Remove from heat, add milk, stir to blend, and return to medium heat. Cook, stirring constantly, until boiling, thickened, and smooth. Turn heat to low and add cheese. Stir until cheese is melted.

LEMON CONSOMMÉ
▼▼▼

½	can (10 oz. or 284 mL size) beef consommé
⅓ cup	water
1 tsp.	lemon juice
½ tsp.	grated lemon rind
1	paper-thin slice lemon

Preparation:
2 minutes
Cooking:
7 minutes

Heat consommé, water, lemon juice, and rind and simmer 5 minutes. Pour into a mug or soup cup and float the slice of lemon on top.

117

PEA AND MUSHROOM POTAGE
▼▼▼

2 tbsp.	butter or margarine
¼ lb.	fresh mushrooms, sliced
1 tbsp.	flour
1½ cups	chicken stock (p. 126)
¼ tsp.	dried leaf chervil
½ cup	frozen peas
¼ tsp.	salt
	Dash pepper
1 cup	2% or skim milk
1	slice onion
1	whole clove
	Small piece bay leaf
1 tbsp.	chopped parsley

Preparation:
10 minutes
Cooking:
15 minutes

Heat 1 tbsp. of the butter or margarine in a medium saucepan. Add mushrooms and cook, stirring, 1 minute. Turn out of pan and set aside. Add remaining butter or margarine to pan, sprinkle in flour, and stir to blend. Remove from heat, add chicken stock and chervil and stir to blend. Return to heat and stir until boiling, thickened, and smooth. Add peas, cover, and simmer 10 minutes.

Put mixture into blender half at a time and blend until smooth. Return to saucepan, add mushrooms, salt, and pepper and heat well. Combine milk, onion slice, clove, bay leaf, and parsley in a small saucepan. Heat to scalding, strain into soup and discard seasonings. Mix well, taste, and adjust seasoning if necessary. Serve very hot.

Makes 2 large servings.

CHEDDAR-ONION SOUP
▼▼▼

½ cup	water
½ tsp.	salt
2	medium potatoes, peeled and sliced
1 tbsp.	butter or margarine
2	medium onions, peeled and sliced
1	large sprig parsley
1	sprig celery leaves
	Dash black pepper
1¼ cups	2% milk
⅓ cup	grated old cheddar cheese
	Chopped parsley

Preparation:
10 minutes
Cooking:
20 minutes

Put water in a medium saucepan and bring to a boil. Add salt and potatoes and bring back to a boil. Reduce heat slightly, cover, and boil until potatoes are tender, about 10 minutes. Do not drain.

Melt butter or margarine in a small skillet over low heat. Add onions and stir until tender but not brown, about 5 minutes. Add to potatoes along with parsley sprig, celery leaves, pepper, and milk. Pour into blender and blend until smooth.

Return to saucepan and heat to scalding (do not boil). Turn heat to low, add cheese, and stir until melted. Serve sprinkled with parsley.

Makes 2 servings.

CREAM OF GREEN ONION SOUP
▼▼▼

8	large green onions (approx.)
½ cup	boiling water
½ tsp.	salt
1 tbsp.	flour
1 tbsp.	soft butter or margarine
	Dash each white pepper and paprika
2 cups	2% milk
	Grated Parmesan cheese

Preparation: 5 minutes
Cooking: 10 minutes

Wash and trim onions, keeping as much of the green tops as possible. Cut them up coarsely and put them in a medium saucepan (there should be about 1 cup). Add boiling water and salt, bring to a boil over medium heat, cover and cook until onions are tender, about 5 minutes.

Pour onions and cooking water into the blender, add flour, butter or margarine, pepper, paprika, and 1 cup of the milk and blend until smooth. Return to saucepan, add remaining milk and heat to scalding (do not boil). Stir in 1 tbsp. Parmesan cheese. Ladle into bowl and sprinkle with more cheese.

Makes 2 servings.

BLENDER VEGETABLE SOUP
▼▼▼

¼	small onion
½	small stalk celery with leaves
½	small carrot
1	sprig parsley
½ cup	tomato juice
¼ cup	water
¼ tsp.	beef stock mix
	Dash Worcestershire sauce
	Tiny dash Tabasco sauce
	Dash pepper

Preparation:
5 minutes
Cooking:
10 minutes

Cut vegetables coarsely into the blender. Add remaining ingredients and blend about 2 seconds (mixture should not be smooth). Pour into small saucepan, bring to a boil, reduce heat, and simmer 10 minutes.

VEGETABLÈ BISQUE
▼▼▼

¾ cup	diced carrots
1 cup	thinly sliced leeks
1 cup	diced potato
1¾ cups	chicken stock (p. 126)
¼ cup	chopped parsley
¼ cup	2% milk
	Dash each salt, pepper, and nutmeg
	Thinly sliced green onion or chopped chives
	Thin strips process cheese slices

Preparation:
10 minutes
Cooking:
20 minutes
Microwave:
13 minutes

Combine carrots, leeks, potato, and chicken stock in a medium saucepan. Bring to a boil, reduce heat, cover, and simmer until vegetables are tender, about 15 minutes. Add parsley and simmer 2 minutes.

Pour into the blender and blend until smooth. Return to saucepan, add milk, and heat well. Taste and season with salt, pepper, and nutmeg. Ladle into bowl and top with green onion or chives and a few strips of cheese.

Makes 2 generous servings.

To microwave: Combine carrots, leeks, potato, and chicken stock in a 2-qt. casserole. Cover and cook at high about 12 minutes, until vegetables are tender. Stir once or twice. Add parsley and cook, covered 30 seconds. Complete as above, reheating in serving bowl in microwave.

SALMON BISQUE
▼▼▼

1	can (3.75 oz. or 106 g size) salmon
1 tbsp.	butter or margarine
1 tbsp.	finely chopped onion
1 tbsp.	finely chopped celery
2 tsp.	flour
¼ tsp.	salt
¼ cup	liquid (salmon liquid plus water)
½ cup	2% milk
¼ cup	tomato juice
2 tsp.	chopped parsley

Preparation:
10 minutes
Cooking:
15 minutes

Drain salmon, saving liquid. Break salmon into small pieces. Heat butter or margarine in a small saucepan, add onion and celery and cook gently, stirring, 5 minutes. Sprinkle in flour and salt and stir to blend. Remove from heat, add the ¼ cup liquid and milk. Stir over medium heat until boiling, thickened, and smooth. Stir in tomato juice and parsley and heat but do not boil. Add salmon and heat well.

LIGHT FISH SOUP
▼▼▼

1	fillet sole, 2 to 3 oz.
1½ cups	water
¼ cup	chopped onion
¼ cup	thin strips carrot
2 tbsp.	chopped celery
¼ tsp.	salt
	Dash white pepper
6 or 8	small shelled and cleaned raw shrimp
¼ cup	skim milk
2 tsp.	cornstarch
1 tsp.	lemon juice
1 tbsp.	chopped parsley
¼ tsp.	dried dill weed or ½ tsp. snipped fresh dill

Preparation:
10 minutes
Cooking:
15 minutes

Let sole thaw slightly at room temperature if using frozen fish. Cut across the fillet in ½-inch squares.

Bring water to a boil in a medium saucepan. Add onion, carrot, celery, salt, and pepper and cook over high heat 5 minutes. Add sole, bring back to a boil, turn heat to medium-low and simmer, uncovered, 2 minutes, stirring carefully from time to time. Add shrimp, cover, and simmer 2 minutes more.

Stir skim milk and cornstarch together until smooth. Gradually stir into simmering mixture, increase temperature enough to get mixture boiling, then reduce again and simmer 2 minutes, stirring carefully. Stir in lemon juice, taste, and adjust seasoning if necessary. Remove from heat, stir in parsley and dill. Makes a generous serving.

CREAMY CHILLED SOUP
▼▼▼

¾ cup	chilled beef or chicken stock (p. 127)
¼ cup	low-fat plain yogurt
½ tsp.	lemon juice
	Dash each garlic salt and black pepper

Preparation:
3 minutes
plus chilling

Combine, pour into mug or soup cup, cover, and chill several hours. This is a satisfying diet soup.

CHICKEN STOCK
▼▼▼

	Chicken bones, wing tips, neck, and giblets (see Four-in-One Chicken p. 56)
4 cups	water
1	small slice onion
	Small piece bay leaf
	Pinch dried leaf thyme
½ tsp.	salt
4	peppercorns
1	small stalk celery with leaves
2	sprigs parsley

Preparation:
5 minutes
Cooking:
2 hours

Put chicken pieces in a large saucepan. Add all remaining ingredients and bring to a boil. Reduce heat, skim, cover, and simmer until meat is falling off bones, about 2 hours.

Strain, discarding bones, vegetables, etc. (All the goodness from the chicken meat will now be in the stock, but if you like, it can be stripped off the bones and returned to the liquid.) Cool the stock quickly by setting in ice water, then refrigerate. Lift off and discard fat and use stock for soup or freeze to use another day.

BASIC STOCK
▼▼▼

This recipe makes a large amount of stock that you can freeze for later use. You can use meat, chicken, or turkey, or a combination.

Preparation:
7 minutes
Cooking:
4 hours

3 or 4 lb.	meat and bones (see note on p. 128)
	Cold water
1	small onion, peeled
1	carrot, scrubbed
2	large celery stalks, with leaves
2	leeks (optional)
2 tsp.	salt
1	bay leaf
4	large sprigs parsley
¼ tsp.	dried leaf thyme
4	peppercorns

Put meat and bones in a large kettle. Cover with cold water to about 2 inches above ingredients. Bring to a boil and skim off any scum. Add coarsely cut-up onion, carrot, celery, and leeks and the seasonings. Reduce heat, cover, and simmer about 4 hours. Strain, discarding bones, vegetables, etc. Cool stock by setting in ice water, then refrigerate. Lift off fat and discard. Use stock immediately or pour it into large jars (leave 1 inch of head space) or tight plastic containers and freeze.

Makes about 10 cups.

Note: Veal bits and bones blend nicely with chicken or turkey bones but keep the other meat bones separate to make their own distinctive stock. For brown stock with a stronger flavor, brown beef meat and bones and the vegetables in a roasting pan in a 450°F oven before putting them in the soup kettle.

VEGETABLES, PASTA & RICE

▼▼▼

VEGETABLES, PASTA, AND RICE
▼▼▼

For me, vegetables are best cooked in a steamer or stir-fried in a skillet or wok. And you'll find most of these recipes use these methods. I think the little collapsible steamers are one of the best inventions ever — and perfect for cooking vegetables for one.

However, some of the following recipes use vegetables in casseroles and in especially interesting ways — for example, Mexican Peppers (p. 149) which suggests stuffing green peppers with a spicy cornmeal mixture and baking them. Another favorite of mine to serve with chicken is Corn Cakes (p. 144). These are really simple little light pancakes.

Useful for those evenings you know you'll be late are Stuffed Baked Potatoes (p. 152). They are prepared ahead and frozen, then you can let one thaw in the refrigerator all day if you wish and heat it in the microwave for only 1 or 2 minutes. Or, if it is still frozen, it can be heated in the regular oven in about 25 minutes.

This section also contains recipes for various noodle and rice dishes that can add interest to an otherwise plain meal.

ASPARAGUS ITALIAN STYLE
▼▼▼

½ cup	fine noodles
1	small clove garlic
½ lb.	fresh asparagus
1 tbsp.	cooking oil
¼ cup	sliced mushrooms
	Dash salt
1 tbsp.	grated Romano or Parmesan cheese

Preparation:
5 minutes
Cooking:
10 to 13
minutes

Cook noodles and garlic in plenty of boiling salted water as directed on noodle package or for about 5 minutes. Drain, discard garlic, and rinse noodles under cold water. Drain again.

Wash asparagus, snap off tough ends and discard. Cut asparagus spears into ½-inch slices on the diagonal, leaving tips whole.

Heat oil in medium skillet. Add asparagus and mushrooms, cover, and cook over medium heat, shaking the pan often, 5 to 8 minutes, or until asparagus is tender-crisp. Add noodles, toss together with a fork until everything is hot, then sprinkle with salt and cheese and serve immediately. Good with fried chicken.

ASPARAGUS CHINESE STYLE
▼▼▼

½ lb.	fresh asparagus
2 tsp.	cooking oil
1	small clove garlic, minced
	Dash salt
1 tsp.	soya sauce

Preparation:
5 minutes
Cooking:
5 to 8
minutes

Wash asparagus and break off and discard tough ends. Cut stalks into 1-inch pieces on the diagonal, leaving tips whole.

Heat oil in medium skillet. Add asparagus, garlic, and salt. Cover and cook over medium-low heat, shaking pan often until asparagus is tender-crisp, 5 to 8 minutes. Stir in soya sauce and serve immediately.

HARVARD BEETS
▼▼▼

½	can (14 oz. or 398 mL size) small whole beets
2 tsp.	sugar
1 tsp.	cornstarch
	Pinch salt
2 tbsp.	beet liquid
1 tbsp.	cider vinegar
¼ tsp.	prepared horseradish
1 tsp.	butter or margarine

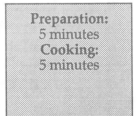

Preparation:
5 minutes
Cooking:
5 minutes

Drain beets, setting aside 2 tbsp. of the liquid. Dice beets.

Combine sugar, cornstarch, and salt in a small saucepan. Stir in beet liquid and vinegar gradually, stirring until smooth. Set over high heat and bring to a boil, stirring constantly. Cook until thick and clear. Reduce heat, stir in horseradish and beets. Heat well, then stir in butter or margarine.

Note: Use remaining beets for Dutch Pickled Beets (p. 135).

134

DUTCH PICKLED BEETS
▼▼▼

½	can (14 oz. or 398 mL size) can small whole beets
3 tbsp.	white vinegar
3 tbsp.	brown sugar
1	small piece stick cinnamon
1	whole clove
	Dash salt

Preparation:
15 minutes

Drain beets, saving ⅓ cup of the liquid (add water if necessary). Pack beets into an 8-oz. jar.

Combine beet liquid with all remaining ingredients in a small saucepan and simmer 10 minutes. Pour over beets. Store in refrigerator for a few days, then enjoy!

BROCCOLI-RICE BAKE
▼▼▼

1½ tsp.	butter or margarine
1 tbsp.	finely chopped onion
1	small clove garlic, crushed
1 cup	chopped cooked broccoli
⅓ cup	cooked rice
2 tbsp.	grated Parmesan cheese
1	egg
3 tbsp.	milk
	Dash each salt and pepper
	Pinch ground nutmeg
¼ cup	grated mozzarella cheese

Preparation:
10 minutes
Cooking:
20 minutes

Heat oven to 350°F. Butter a shallow baking dish about 8 x 6 x 2 inches. Melt butter or margarine in a medium skillet over medium heat and add onion and garlic. Stir 3 minutes, remove from heat and add cooked broccoli, rice, and Parmesan cheese. Toss together lightly with a fork and turn into prepared baking dish.

Beat egg, milk, salt, pepper, and nutmeg together with a fork and pour over broccoli mixture, pressing broccoli down into egg mixture. Sprinkle with mozzarella cheese.

Bake 15 to 20 minutes or until set. Good to serve with fish or chicken.

BROCCOLI WITH YOGURT SAUCE
▼▼▼

¼ cup	plain low-fat yogurt
½ tsp.	lemon juice
	Pinch sugar
	Pinch salt
¼ tsp.	finely chopped green onion
1	medium stalk broccoli
	Grating fresh pepper
2 tsp.	butter or margarine
1 tbsp.	toasted slivered almonds
½ tsp.	chopped pimento

Preparation:
10 minutes
Cooking:
5 minutes
Standing:
1 hour

Combine yogurt, lemon juice, sugar, salt, and onion and let stand at least 1 hour.

Cut tough bottom stems and leaves from broccoli and discard. Cut off flowers and break them into small sections. Cut stems into cubes. Cook in a small amount of boiling water or in a steamer until just tender, about 5 minutes. Drain.

Grate a little pepper over the hot broccoli, add the butter or margarine and toss lightly. Add almonds and pimento to yogurt mixture and serve over hot broccoli.

137

SCALLOPED CABBAGE
▼▼▼

¼	small cabbage
	Boiling water
	Dash salt
	Pinch sugar
1 tbsp.	butter or margarine
1 tbsp.	flour
	Dash each salt and pepper
	Pinch ground mace
¾ cup	2% milk
3 tbsp.	grated old cheddar cheese
2 tbsp.	fine dry bread crumbs
2 tsp.	butter or margarine

Preparation:
7 minutes
Cooking:
25 minutes

Heat oven to 400°F. Grease a small casserole, about 2 cup size.

Cut cabbage coarsely. You will have 2 to 2½ cups. Put cabbage in a small saucepan, cover with boiling water, and add dash salt and pinch sugar. Bring to a boil, cover, and cook until barely tender, about 5 minutes. Drain well and put in prepared casserole.

Melt 1 tbsp. butter or margarine in small saucepan. Sprinkle in flour, dash salt, pepper, and mace and stir to blend. Remove from heat and stir in milk. Return to medium heat and stir until boiling, thickened, and smooth. Reduce heat and simmer 2 minutes, then pour over cabbage. Mix cheese and bread crumbs and sprinkle over all. Dot with 2 tsp. butter or margarine. Bake about 15 minutes or until crumbs are lightly browned and mixture is hot.

SPANISH CARROTS
▼▼▼

2	medium carrots
1 tbsp.	butter or margarine
½	small clove garlic, crushed
1 tbsp.	water
	Dash salt
2 tbsp.	thin strips green pepper
2 tsp.	ketchup
	Dash chili powder

Preparation:
5 minutes
Cooking:
8 minutes

Cut carrots in thin slices on the diagonal. Heat butter or margarine in a small saucepan just until it begins to brown. Add garlic and carrots and stir. Add water, cover tightly, and cook over highest heat, lifting lid and stirring several times and adding a little water if necessary, 4 minutes or until carrots are beginning to get tender. Sprinkle in salt and add green pepper. Cover and cook 2 minutes or until everything is tender-crisp. Turn off heat and stir in ketchup and chili powder.

GLAZED BABY CARROTS
▼▼▼

1 cup	whole baby carrots (fresh or frozen)
2 tsp.	butter or margarine
1 tsp.	sugar
¼ tsp.	dry mustard
2 tsp.	orange juice
	Grating fresh pepper

Preparation: 3 minutes
Cooking: 10 minutes

Cook carrots in a steamer until barely tender.

Melt butter or margarine in a small saucepan. Blend sugar, mustard, and orange juice and stir into butter. Add carrots, cover and heat over low heat 2 to 3 minutes, shaking the pan often, or until carrots are hot and lightly glazed. Grate pepper over all.

CREAMY DILLED CAULIFLOWER
▼▼▼

1 cup	small cauliflower flowerets
1 tbsp.	butter or margarine
1 tbsp.	flour
	Dash each salt and pepper
¾ cup	milk
⅓ cup	grated old cheddar cheese
¼ tsp.	dried dill weed or ½ tsp. snipped fresh dill

Preparation:
10 minutes
Cooking:
10 minutes

Cook cauliflower until barely tender in steamer or a small amount of boiling water, 4 to 5 minutes.

Heat butter or margarine in a small saucepan. Stir in flour, salt, and pepper, remove from heat and stir in milk. Return to medium heat and stir until boiling, thickened, and smooth. Stir in cheese and dill and add cooked cauliflower. Stir gently just until hot.

CELERY AND CORN IN SAUCE
▼▼▼

½ cup	celery, cut in thin slices on diagonal
¼ cup	boiling water
¾ tsp.	cornstarch
1 tbsp.	cold water
½ cup	whole kernel corn
	Pinch salt
	Grating fresh pepper
	Pinch dried leaf savory

Preparation:
5 minutes
Cooking:
5 minutes

Cook celery in boiling water in a small saucepan over medium heat until tender-crisp, about 3 minutes. Do not drain.

Mix cornstarch and cold water and stir into boiling mixture gradually. Stir until thick and clear, then stir in remaining ingredients and heat gently 2 minutes.

BUTTERED CELERY AND ONION

2 tsp.	butter or margarine
½ cup	thinly sliced celery
½ cup	thin slices onion, separated into rings
¼ cup	thin strips green pepper
1 tbsp.	water
	Dash each salt and pepper
⅛ tsp.	caraway seeds

> **Preparation:**
> 7 minutes
> **Cooking:**
> 5 minutes

Heat butter or margarine in medium skillet. Add celery, onion rings, green pepper, and water. Cover and cook over medium-high heat, stirring occasionally, just until vegetables are tender-crisp, about 3 minutes. Sprinkle with seasonings.

CORN CAKES
▼▼▼

1	cob cooked corn (or ½ cup canned whole kernel corn)
2 tsp.	melted butter or margarine
1 tbsp.	light cream
1	egg yolk
	Dash each salt and pepper
	Dash ground nutmeg
1	egg white

Preparation:
5 minutes
Cooking:
5 minutes

Cut corn from cob and mix with remaining ingredients except egg white. Beat egg white until stiff with a wire whip or egg beater. Fold into corn mixture (the mixture will be very thin).

Drop by heaping tablespoonfuls on a hot greased griddle or heavy skillet, spreading into cakes about 3 inches in diameter. Brown on one side, then turn carefully and brown second side. Makes about 6 small cakes. Especially good with chicken or ham.

BUTTER-STEAMED LEEKS
▼▼▼

1	slice bacon
2 tsp.	butter or margarine
1 cup	thinly sliced leeks (white and pale green parts)
1½ tbsp.	water
	Salt and pepper

Preparation:
5 minutes
Cooking:
5 minutes

Fry bacon in skillet until crisp, drain on paper towelling, and crumble.

Drain fat from skillet and add butter or margarine. Heat over medium-high heat. Add leeks and water, stir, and cover tightly. Cook quickly, stirring often and adding a little more water if necessary, until leeks are just tender, about 3 minutes. Sprinkle lightly with salt and pepper, add bacon bits and toss with a fork.

DILLED ONIONS
▼▼▼

4	small onions
1 tsp.	butter or margarine
2 tbsp.	tomato juice
1 tbsp.	brown sugar
	Dash salt
	Dash paprika
¼ tsp.	dried dill weed or ½ tsp. snipped fresh dill

Preparation:
5 minutes
Cooking:
20 minutes
Microwave:
5 minutes

Heat oven to 350°F. Grease a small casserole, about 2 cup size.

Peel onions and put them in a small saucepan. Cover with boiling water and boil 10 minutes. Drain and put in prepared casserole. Combine remaining ingredients and pour over onions. Cover and bake about 10 minutes or until tender.

To microwave: Put onions and tomato juice in small microwave-safe dish. Cover and microwave at high 3 minutes. Add remaining ingredients and cover again. Microwave 1 minute, stir, and microwave 1 minute more. Let stand 5 minutes.

PEAS FRENCH STYLE

1	large outside leaf iceberg lettuce
1 cup	fresh or frozen peas
2	white bulbs from green onions
	Pinch sugar
2 tsp.	water
	Pinch salt
	Grating fresh pepper
2 tsp.	butter or margarine
1 tbsp.	light cream

Preparation:
5 minutes
Cooking:
6 minutes

Rinse lettuce and use to line a small saucepan. Add peas, onions, sugar, and water. Cover tightly and cook over medium heat until peas are just tender, about 5 minutes. Remove and discard lettuce, add remaining ingredients, and heat over low heat for a few seconds.

CHINESE PEAS AND MUSHROOMS
▼▼▼

1	thin slice packaged cooked ham
¼ tsp.	chicken stock mix
⅓ cup	boiling water
1½ tsp.	cornstarch
3 tbsp.	cold water
2 tsp.	cooking oil
½ cup	sliced fresh mushrooms
½ cup	frozen peas
¼ cup	cut-up bamboo shoots (optional)
¼ tsp.	salt

Preparation:
7 minutes
Cooking:
5 minutes

Cut ham into short narrow strips. Dissolve stock mix in boiling water. Combine cornstarch and cold water in a small dish.

Heat oil in heavy skillet or wok over high heat. Add ham and mushrooms and cook quickly 1 minute, stirring. Add frozen peas, bamboo shoots, salt, and chicken stock. Cook quickly 1 minute, stirring. Stir in cornstarch mixture gradually, using just enough to make a slightly thickened sauce. Good with noodles for a lunch dish.

MEXICAN PEPPERS
▼▼▼

1 tsp.	cooking oil
2 tbsp.	chopped onion
⅔ cup	canned tomatoes with juice
3 tbsp.	cornmeal
¼ tsp.	salt
¾ tsp.	chili powder
2 tbsp.	slivered ripe olives
⅓ cup	cooked fresh corn, cut from cob
¼ cup	grated cheddar cheese
2	medium green peppers
1 tbsp.	grated cheddar cheese
2 tbsp.	water

Preparation:
10 minutes
Cooking:
40 minutes
Microwave
10 minutes

Heat oven to 350 °F. Have ready a small shallow baking dish that will just hold the peppers.

Heat oil in a small heavy saucepan. Add onion and cook gently 3 minutes. Add tomatoes (break or cut up large pieces) and heat to boiling. Stir in cornmeal, salt, and chili powder and cook over medium-low heat, stirring, until thick, about 5 minutes. Remove and stir in olives, corn, and ¼ cup cheese.

Cut tops from peppers and remove ribs and seeds. Drop in boiling water to cover and boil gently 5 minutes. Drain.

Put peppers in baking dish and fill with cornmeal mixture. Sprinkle with 1 tbsp. cheese. Add about 2 tbsp. water to baking dish and bake 30 minutes or until peppers are tender.

To microwave: Combine oil and onion in a small microwave-safe dish or glass measuring cup. Cover with waxed paper and microwave at high 1 minute.

Stir in tomatoes and heat to boiling in microwave, about 1½ minutes. Stir in cornmeal, salt, and chili powder, cover with waxed paper and microwave at high 1½ to 2 minutes, stirring every 30 seconds, or until very thick. Remove from microwave and stir in olives, corn, and ¼ cup cheese.

Cut tops from peppers and remove ribs and seeds. Put in small microwave-safe baking dish and fill with cornmeal mixture. Add 2 tbsp. water to dish, cover tightly, and microwave at high about 6 minutes, turning ½ turn after 3 minutes or when beginning to get tender. Uncover, sprinkle with the 1 tbsp. cheese, cover again, and let stand 5 minutes.

These are especially good to serve with pork chops or fried chicken.

HERBED PEPPERS
▼▼▼

1	small red pepper
1	small green pepper
1 tbsp.	olive oil
1 tsp.	wine vinegar
	Pinch salt
⅛ tsp.	dried leaf oregano
	Generous grating fresh pepper

Preparation:
5 minutes
Cooking:
5 minutes

Cut peppers in half lengthwise, remove ribs and seeds, and cut each half into 4 lengthwise strips.

Heat oil in medium skillet and add peppers. Cook over medium heat, stirring, about 5 minutes, or until just barely tender. They should be crisp and still have their bright color. Stir in remaining ingredients and serve immediately. Or chill and serve as salad.

151

STUFFED BAKED POTATOES
▼▼▼

This is a handy freezer recipe.
Cooked four at a time but frozen
individually, these potatoes
provide a quick,tasty addition
to your meal.

Preparation:
15 minutes
Cooking:
1 hour
Heating:
20 - 25 minutes

4	large baking potatoes
	Melted butter
	or margarine
⅓ cup	hot milk
2 tbsp.	soft butter
	or margarine
¼ tsp.	salt
⅛ tsp.	pepper
¼ tsp.	garlic salt
3 tbsp.	grated Swiss cheese

Heat oven to 400 °F. Scrub potatoes very well and prick each in a few places on the top only. Put on baking sheet and bake about 1 hour or until tender.

Cut a thin slice from the tops of the potatoes where they were pricked. Discard slices and scoop pulp out of potatoes carefully with a spoon into a bowl, leaving about ¼ inch of potato inside the skins to make shells to hold the filling. Set these shells back on baking sheet and brush all over inside with melted butter or margarine. Return to oven for about 7 minutes to crisp the shells and make them nice and firm.

Beat hot potato pulp, milk, 2 tbsp. butter or margarine, salt, pepper, and garlic salt with electric mixer or rotary beater until smooth and fluffy. Spoon into potato shells.

152

Brush tops lightly with melted butter or margarine and sprinkle with grated cheese.

Set potatoes on cardboard and wrap tightly in foil, or put them in a rigid freezer container and freeze.

When ready to bake, heat oven to 400 °F. Put a potato on a small baking sheet and bake 20 to 25 minutes or until very hot and lightly browned.

To heat in microwave: *Thaw first,* then heat 1 minute per potato. Or if directly from refrigerator increase time by ½ minute per potato.

POTATO CAKES
▼▼▼

1 tbsp.	finely chopped onion
1 tsp.	cooking oil
1 cup	leftover mashed potatoes
1 tbsp.	melted butter or margarine
¼ tsp.	salt
	Dash pepper
1	egg white
	Flour
1 tbsp.	butter or margarine

Preparation:
5 minutes
Cooking:
15 minutes

Fry onion in oil in a small skillet until transparent, about 3 minutes. Whip potatoes (use mixer or a wire whip), 1 tbsp. melted butter or margarine, salt, pepper, and egg white until fluffy. Blend in onion. Mixture will be quite soft.

Shape mixture into 2 large, thick cakes and dip each side of cakes into flour to coat well.

Heat 1 tbsp. butter or margarine in same skillet used for onion and fry cakes over medium heat until well browned on both sides. (Be sure to brown first side until *crusty* brown to make turning easy.)

QUICK SCALLOPED POTATOES
▼▼▼

2 tsp.	butter or margarine
1	small onion, sliced
1½ cups	thinly sliced cooked potatoes
2 tbsp.	grated old cheddar cheese
	Salt and pepper
¼ cup	plain low-fat yogurt
	Paprika

Preparation:
10 minutes
Cooking:
20 minutes
Microwave:
7 minutes

Heat butter or margarine in a small skillet. Add onion and cook gently 3 minutes, stirring.

Heat oven to 350 °F. Butter a small casserole, about 2 cup size. Layer potatoes, onion, and cheese in casserole (2 layers each), sprinkling each potato layer lightly with salt and pepper. Spread yogurt over top and sprinkle with paprika. Bake about 20 minutes.

To microwave: Prepare as above and cover. Microwave at high for about 7 minutes, turning ½ turn after 3 minutes. Let stand 5 minutes.

155

OVEN-FRIED POTATOES
▼▼▼

1 tbsp.	olive oil
1	small clove garlic, cut in half
2 tbsp.	chopped parsley
¼ tsp.	dried leaf savory
¼ tsp.	dried leaf thyme
1	medium-size potato, peeled and cut into 8 equal pieces
	Salt and pepper

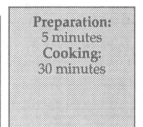

Preparation:
5 minutes
Cooking:
30 minutes

Heat oven to 400 °F. Have ready a small metal pan (an 8-inch cake pan or loaf pan will do).

Heat oil and garlic in the metal pan in the oven 3 minutes, stirring once. Remove from oven and discard garlic. Add parsley, savory, and thyme to the pan and stir. Add potato pieces and stir them around so they are coated with the herb mixture and oil. Sprinkle lightly with salt and pepper. Cover pan with foil.

Bake about 25 minutes or until tender and lightly browned, stirring after first 15 minutes.

SWEET POTATO WITH MAPLE SYRUP
▼▼▼

1	sweet potato
1 tbsp.	maple syrup
2 tsp.	butter or margarine
¼ tsp.	grated orange rind

Preparation:
3 minutes
Cooking:
40 to 70 minutes
Microwave:
14 to 16 minutes

Boil (30 to 35 minutes), bake (50 to 60 minutes at 350°F) or microwave (4 to 6 minutes at high) sweet potato until tender.

Peel and cut into 2 or 3 thick slices. Heat syrup, butter or margarine, and orange rind in a small skillet. Add potato slices in a single layer, cover, and heat over medium-low heat until potato is hot and glazed, about 10 minutes, turning once during heating.

CORN-STUFFED TOMATO
▼▼▼

1	large tomato
	Salt
1	small cob cooked corn (or ⅓ cup canned whole kernel corn)
1 tbsp.	chopped green pepper
	Tiny pinch anise seed (optional)
2 tsp.	fine dry bread crumbs
1 tsp.	melted butter or margarine
2 tsp.	grated old cheddar cheese

> **Preparation:**
> 10 minutes
> **Cooking:**
> 15 minutes
> **Microwave:**
> 2 minutes

Heat oven to 350 °F. Have ready a small baking dish or custard cup that will just hold the tomato.

Cut stem end from tomato and discard. Scoop out center of tomato, leaving a thick wall to hold the filling. (Save the center to add to soup, sauce, or a casserole.) Sprinkle inside of tomato lightly with salt and invert on paper towel to drain.

Cut corn from cob and combine with green pepper and anise seed. Pile into tomato shell and set in baking dish. Combine crumbs, butter or margarine, and cheese and sprinkle on top.

Bake until tomato is tender and topping is lightly browned, about 15 minutes.

To microwave: Prepare according to directions above. Cover and microwave on high 1 minute, turn ½ turn and microwave 1 minute. Let stand covered 3 minutes.

TURNIP CASSEROLE
▼▼▼

1 cup	¾-inch cubes turnip (rutabaga)
2 tsp.	butter or margarine
¼ cup	chopped green pepper
1 tsp.	finely chopped onion
1 tsp.	flour
	Dash each salt and pepper
2 tbsp.	chili sauce
1 tbsp.	water
2 tbsp.	grated Swiss cheese

Preparation:
10 minutes
Cooking:
40 minutes

Boil turnip cubes until tender, about 20 minutes.

Heat oven to 350 °F. Butter a small casserole, about 2 cup size. Heat 2 tsp. butter or margarine in a small saucepan. Add green pepper and onion and cook gently, stirring, until onion is very lightly browned. Sprinkle in flour, salt, and pepper and stir to blend. Remove from heat and add chili sauce and water, stir to blend, and return to medium heat. Stir until thickened. Stir in cooked turnip and turn into prepared casserole. Sprinkle with cheese.

Bake about 15 minutes or until cheese is melted and mixture is very hot.

ZUCCHINI AND PEPPERS
▼▼▼

1	slice bacon, cut in 1-inch squares
¼ cup	thinly sliced onion
½	small red pepper, cut in short ¼-inch wide strips
½	small green pepper, cut in short ¼-inch wide strips
1	small zucchini sliced ½ inch thick
	Dash each salt and pepper
	Pinch dried leaf thyme

Preparation:
10 minutes
Cooking:
15 minutes

Cook bacon in a medium skillet until crisp. Lift out pieces with a slotted spoon and drain on paper towelling.

Add onion to drippings in pan and cook gently, stirring, 5 minutes. Add a few drops of oil if necessary. Add red and green pepper strips and zucchini. Sprinkle with seasonings. Cover and cook over medium heat, shaking the pan often, until vegetables are tender-crisp, about 5 minutes. Add bacon bits. Good with fish or chicken.

BACON NOODLES
▼▼▼

2	slices bacon
½	small clove garlic, minced
1 cup	medium noodles
	Dash black pepper
	Pinch ground nutmeg
¼ cup	chopped parsley (Italian if possible)
2 tbsp.	grated Parmesan cheese

Preparation:
5 minutes
Cooking:
8 to 10 minutes

Fry bacon until crisp, then drain on paper towelling, cool and crumble. Discard all but about 2 tsp. bacon fat, then add garlic to pan and stir over medium heat 3 minutes. Do not brown. Remove from heat.

Cook noodles until just tender in plenty of boiling salted water, about 5 minutes. Drain and return to pan. Add pepper, nutmeg, and crumbled bacon. Reheat any bacon fat left in pan, stir in parsley, and pour over hot noodles. Toss with two forks and sprinkle with Parmesan cheese.

FETTUCINE

1 cup	**medium noodles**
2 tbsp.	**unsalted butter, cut in small pieces**
¼ cup	**grated Parmesan cheese (fresh Italian if possible)**
¼ cup	**light cream**
	Dash pepper

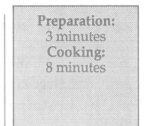

Preparation:
3 minutes
Cooking:
8 minutes

Cook noodles in plenty of boiling water until just tender, about 5 minutes. Drain and return to pan. Set over lowest heat, add remaining ingredients and stir gently just until butter, cheese, and cream melt into a smooth sauce and coat the noodles.

CREAMY NOODLES
▼▼▼

1¼ cups	medium noodles (2 oz.)
½ cup	finely torn-up fresh spinach (packed in cup)
3 tbsp.	cream-style cottage cheese
1 tbsp.	plain yogurt or sour cream
1 tbsp.	dry white wine
1	large green onion with top, finely chopped
¼ tsp.	salt
	Grating fresh pepper
	Dash ground nutmeg
1 tbsp.	grated Parmesan cheese
1½ tsp.	butter or margarine

Preparation:
7 minutes
Cooking:
22 minutes

Heat oven to 375 °F. Butter a small casserole, about 2 cup size.

Cook noodles in plenty of boiling salted water 5 minutes. Add spinach and cook 2 minutes. Drain immediately.

Combine cottage cheese, yogurt or sour cream, wine, onion, salt, pepper, and nutmeg, then stir in drained noodle mixture. Turn into prepared casserole, sprinkle with Parmesan cheese, and dot with butter or margarine. Bake about 15 minutes or until very hot.

163

CURRIED NOODLES
▼▼▼

1 cup	medium noodles
1 tbsp.	butter or margarine
¼ cup	canned sliced mushrooms, drained
1 tbsp.	minced onion
½	small clove garlic, minced
¾ tsp.	curry powder
⅛ tsp.	mustard seeds
¼ tsp.	chicken stock mix
½ cup	boiling water
⅛ tsp.	ground ginger
	Small pinch crushed dry red pepper
1 tbsp.	cold water
1½ tsp.	cornstarch
3 tbsp.	plain yogurt
	Chopped parsley

Preparation:
10 minutes
Cooking:
15 to 18
minutes

Cook noodles in plenty of boiling salted water until just tender, 5 to 7 minutes. Drain and set aside.

Heat butter or margarine in a medium saucepan over medium heat. Add mushrooms, onion, garlic, curry powder, and mustard seeds and stir 3 minutes. Add chicken stock mix, boiling water, ginger, and dry red pepper and bring to a boil.

Combine cold water and cornstarch, blending until smooth. Gradually stir into boiling liquid and stir until boiling, thickened, and smooth. Add cooked noodles and

164

heat well. Stir in yogurt and heat but do not boil. Sprinkle with parsley and serve immediately. Especially good with chicken.

MICROWAVING PASTA

To microwave ½ cup macaroni

Put ½ cup uncooked macaroni in a 1-qt. casserole. Add 1½ cups boiling water and ½ tsp. salt, stir, then microwave on high, uncovered, about 4 minutes. Stir once during cooking. Remove from oven, cover tightly, and let stand 10 minutes. Drain and serve. Makes 1 cup cooked.

To microwave 1 cup medium noodles

Put 2 cups hot water, 1 tsp. cooking oil, ½ tsp. salt, and 1 cup medium noodles in a 1½-qt. casserole. Microwave on high, uncovered, 5 minutes, stirring after 3 minutes. Remove from oven, cover tightly, and let stand 5 minutes. Drain.

MEXICAN RICE
▼▼▼

1 tbsp.	cooking oil
⅓ cup	long grain rice
1 tbsp.	chopped onion
½	small clove garlic, minced
2	canned whole green chilies, drained, seeded, and finely chopped
	Pinch salt
1 cup	chicken stock (p. 126)
¼ cup	frozen peas
1 tbsp.	chopped parsley
1 tbsp.	chopped pimento

Preparation:
10 minutes
Cooking:
30 minutes

Heat oil in medium saucepan. Add rice, onion, and garlic and cook and stir until rice is golden. Drain off any excess oil. Add chopped chilies, salt, and chicken stock. Bring to a boil, reduce heat, cover, and simmer 20 minutes. Add peas and continue cooking until rice is tender and liquid is absorbed, about 5 minutes more. Add parsley and pimento and toss with a fork.

Note: Mexican ingredients are available in most supermarkets now. The canned peppers vary greatly in hotness. The chilies I used when testing this recipe were only mildly hot, so I used two. Use less if the chilies you use are very hot. It's a good idea to remove the seeds from peppers since much of the hotness is in them. The rice, however, should have a definite "heat" to it. Use 1 cup water and ½ tsp. chicken stock mix in place of stock if desired.

MUSHROOM PILAF
▼▼▼

1 tbsp.	butter or margarine
⅓ cup	sliced fresh mushrooms
½	small clove garlic, crushed
3 tbsp.	uncooked long grain rice
½ cup	boiling water
¼ tsp.	chicken stock mix
	Pinch dried leaf thyme
	Dash each salt and pepper

Preparation:
7 minutes
Cooking:
25 minutes

Heat butter or margarine in small skillet and add mushrooms, garlic, and rice. Stir over medium heat until rice is golden. Add water, stock mix, and seasonings. Reduce heat to low, cover, and simmer until rice is tender, about 20 minutes, then check for doneness. (Do not uncover during cooking.) If the water is not completely absorbed, cook uncovered for 2 or 3 minutes.

Note: To vary this recipe, add your choice of finely sliced vegetables to the skillet with the mushrooms.

TO COOK RICE

If you are fond of rice, I recommend that you cook 1 cup at a time, then store it in the refrigerator or freezer to reheat as is or add to casseroles.

1 cup	uncooked rice (regular, parboiled, or brown)
2 cups	liquid for regular rice or 2½ cups for parboiled or brown rice
½ tsp.	salt

Combine ingredients in a medium saucepan. Bring to a boil, stir with a fork, turn heat to low, and cover pan tightly. Cook over low heat 15 minutes for regular rice, 20 to 25 minutes for parboiled rice, and 45 minutes for brown rice. Do not lift lid during this cooking time. However, if at the end of cooking time rice is not quite tender or liquid is not absorbed, cook a few minutes longer with lid tilted slightly.

To reheat, put rice in a saucepan, add a small amount of water, cover tightly, and set over low heat until hot, 5 minutes or so.

To microwave:

1 cup	uncooked rice (regular, parboiled, or brown)
2¼ cups	hot liquid for regular or parboiled rice or 3 cups plus 1 tbsp. cooking oil for brown rice
½ tsp.	salt

Put all ingredients in a 3-qt. casserole and cover tightly. For regular or parboiled rice, cook at high 18 to 21 minutes, stirring after 10 minutes. For brown rice, cook at high 30 to 35 minutes, stirring after 20 minutes.

To reheat, put rice in a microwave-safe dish or on a serving plate, cover tightly with transparent wrap, and heat at high a minute or so.

Note: Liquid for cooking rice may be water, chicken stock, meat stock, vegetable cooking water, or even fruit juice.

SALADS & DRESSINGS

▼▼▼

SALADS AND DRESSINGS
▼▼▼

All of us know that leafy green vegetables are good for us. But even if they weren't, I'm sure we'd all want to eat salad regularly. What adds more to a meal than a crisp salad with a good dressing?

There is wide choice of salad recipes here — green salads, vegetable salads, and slaws. Salads that can make a whole meal are very good and very useful, especially in the summer, and some suggested here use beef strips, diced and slivered ham, chicken, or fish to add protein to the goodness of the vegetables. Dressings are very varied and include some that are good for the diet conscious.

CHEF'S SALAD
▼▼▼

1 cup	torn-up lettuce
3 tbsp.	finely grated carrot (1 small)
2	green onions, sliced paper thin
	Yogurt Dressing (p. 205)
	Lettuce
¼ cup	julienne strips cooked chicken or ham
¼ cup	julienne strips Swiss cheese
4	small sardines

Preparation:
10 minutes
plus chilling

Combine torn-up lettuce, carrot, and onions in a shallow bowl. Cover and chill. At serving time toss the vegetables with enough Yogurt Dressing to moisten. Line a small salad bowl with lettuce, pile in the salad, and arrange chicken or ham, cheese, and sardines on top.

FRESH SPINACH SALAD
▼▼▼

1	strip bacon
2 cups	torn-up fresh spinach (pack lightly to measure)
¼ cup	fresh alfalfa sprouts
1	hard-cooked egg, chopped (p. 105)
	Grating fresh pepper
	Zesty Dressing (p. 206)

Preparation:
10 minutes

Fry bacon until crisp, drain on paper towelling and crumble. Combine all ingredients in a bowl and toss with enough of the Zesty Dressing to just coat the spinach.

CUCUMBER SALAD

½	medium English cucumber
2 tbsp.	commercial Italian salad dressing
1 tbsp.	slivered ripe olives
1 tbsp.	capers, chopped
¼ tsp.	snipped fresh dill
	Lettuce

Preparation:
7 minutes
plus chilling

Wash cucumber and run tines of a fork down the length to score through the skin. Slice very thinly. Put in bowl, add all remaining ingredients except lettuce and toss. Chill well and serve on lettuce.

174

GREEN BEAN SALAD
▼▼▼

2 tbsp.	olive oil
2 tsp.	wine vinegar
	Dash each salt and pepper
½	small clove garlic
1 cup	frenched fresh green beans
¼ cup	thin slices radishes
¼ cup	chopped red onion
	Lettuce

Preparation:
10 minutes
plus chilling

Combine oil, vinegar, salt, pepper, and garlic in a small jar with a tight lid. Shake to blend well and let stand at least 1 hour. Discard garlic. Cook beans in a small amount of water or in a steamer about 5 minutes or until tender-crisp. Chill by running under cold water. Drain well, then combine with radishes and onion. Pour oil mixture over vegtables, toss, and chill well. Serve on lettuce.

MARINATED VEGETABLE SALAD
▼▼▼

½ cup	cooked mixed vegetables (use leftovers or frozen mixture)
1 tbsp.	finely chopped onion
1 tbsp.	sugar
1 tbsp.	wine vinegar
1½ tbsp.	olive oil
	Pinch dried leaf oregano
	Pinch curry powder
	Dash pepper
	Lettuce

Preparation:
5 minutes
plus chilling

Combine cooked vegetables and onion in a bowl. Shake remaining ingredients, except lettuce, in a small jar with a tight lid. Pour over vegetables, cover, and chill several hours. Drain at serving time and spoon onto lettuce.

MUSHROOM-SNOW PEA SALAD
▼▼▼

1 tbsp.	olive oil
1 tsp.	cider vinegar
1 tsp.	lemon juice
¼ tsp.	soya sauce
½	small clove garlic
½ tsp.	very finely chopped candied or preserved ginger
12	fresh snow peas (Chinese pea pods)
4	large fresh mushrooms
¼ cup	short slivers sweet red pepper
	Lettuce
1 tsp.	toasted sesame seeds (optional)

Preparation:
15 minutes
plus chilling

Combine oil, vinegar, lemon juice, soya sauce, garlic, and ginger in a small jar with a tight lid and shake to blend well. Chill several hours. Discard garlic.

Steam peas about 3 minutes or until barely tender, then chill. Slice mushrooms paper thin.

Combine peas, mushrooms, and red pepper slivers in a bowl and pour dressing over. Toss gently, cover tightly, and chill. Spoon onto lettuce at serving time and sprinkle with sesame seeds.

CHOPPED TOMATO SALAD
▼▼▼

1	medium tomato, peeled, seeded, and diced
½	small green pepper, diced
¼ cup	diced celery
¼ cup	chopped Spanish onion
1½ tbsp.	lime juice
	Generous grating fresh pepper
	Lettuce

Preparation:
10 minutes
plus chilling

Combine all ingredients except lettuce, tossing lightly. Cover and chill well. Drain and serve on lettuce.

MINTED TOMATO AND ONION SALAD

1	**medium tomato, sliced ¼ inch thick**
3	**thin slices small Spanish onion (see note)**
2 tbsp.	**French Dressing (p. 200)**
½ tsp.	**chopped fresh mint**
	Lettuce
	Sprig mint

Preparation:
5 minutes
plus chilling

Overlap tomato and onion slices in flat dish. Drizzle the French Dressing over and sprinkle with chopped mint. Let stand in refrigerator several hours.

Serve on lettuce garnished with mint sprig.

Note: If the Spanish onion is large, use half slices.

179

GOLDEN SLAW
▼▼▼

1 cup	**finely shredded cabbage**
⅓ cup	**diced unpeeled apple**
¼ cup	**slivered Swiss cheese**
	Dash each salt and pepper
1 tbsp.	**mayonnaise**
1½ tsp.	**prepared mustard**

**Preparation:
10 minutes
plus chilling**

Toss cabbage, apple, cheese, salt, and pepper together in a bowl and chill. Combine mayonnaise and mustard and toss with cabbage at serving time.

PEPPER SLAW
▼▼▼

2 tsp.	soft butter or margarine
2 tsp.	flour
¼ tsp.	sugar
¼ tsp.	dry mustard
	Dash each salt and white pepper
1	egg yolk
2 tsp.	white vinegar
¼ cup	light cream
¾ cup	finely shredded cabbage
2 tbsp.	diced red pepper
2 tbsp.	diced green pepper
2 tbsp.	diced celery

Preparation:
15 minutes
plus chilling

Beat butter or margarine, flour, sugar, mustard, salt, pepper, egg yolk, and vinegar together in a small saucepan until blended. Stir in cream and set over medium heat. Stir until thickened and smooth. Remove from heat. Put cabbage, red and green pepper, and celery in a bowl and add the warm cream mixture. Toss lightly, then cover and refrigerate, chilling at least 2 hours before serving. (This, like most slaws, is still very good after being refrigerated 48 hours.)

RICE SALAD
▼▼▼

1 tsp.	olive oil
½ tsp.	wine vinegar
¼ tsp.	curry powder
2 tsp.	commercial chutney (chop any large pieces)
4	cherry tomatoes, quartered
2 tbsp.	thin strips green pepper
½ cup	cooked rice (p. 168)
	Salt and pepper
	Lettuce

Preparation:
7 minutes
plus chilling

Mix oil, vinegar, curry powder, and chutney in a bowl. Add tomatoes, green pepper, and rice and toss with a fork. Taste and add salt and pepper as needed. Chill well and serve on lettuce.

COTTAGE CHEESE-POTATO SALAD
▼▼▼

1	large potato (preferably new), scrubbed
1 tbsp.	salad oil
1 tsp.	white vinegar
¼ tsp.	salt
¼ cup	thinly sliced celery
1 tbsp.	finely chopped green pepper
1 tbsp.	finely chopped pimento
1 tbsp.	slivered ripe olives
1	small green onion, thinly sliced
1 tbsp.	mayonnaise
⅓ cup	low-fat cottage cheese
	Lettuce

Preparation:
30 minutes
including cooking
potato
plus chilling

Cook potato in its jacket until just tender. Cool until it can be handled (but still hot), peel, and dice into a bowl. You should have about 1 cup. Stir oil, vinegar, and salt together and pour over hot potato, tossing lightly. Cool.

Add celery, green pepper, pimento, olives, and onion. Stir mayonnaise and cottage cheese together, add to salad, and toss lightly. Chill well. Serve on lettuce.

VEGETABLE-BEEF SALAD
▼▼▼

½ cup	match-like strips leftover roast beef
½ cup	diced cold cooked potatoes
1 tsp.	grated onion
¼ cup	finely chopped celery
1½ tbsp.	French Dressing (p. 200)
¼ tsp.	salt
	Dash pepper
1	hard-cooked egg, chopped (p. 105)
4	cherry tomatoes, halved
1 tbsp.	mayonnaise
	Lettuce

Preparation:
15 minutes
plus chilling

Combine beef strips, diced potatoes, onion, celery, French Dressing, salt, and pepper and toss together with a fork. Cover and chill at least 1 hour. Add egg, tomatoes, and mayonnaise and toss together lightly at serving time. Spoon onto lettuce.

HAM AND EGG SALAD
▼▼▼

½ cup	cooked peas
¼ cup	thinly sliced celery
1 tbsp.	chopped green pepper
2 tsp.	finely chopped green onion
1 tbsp.	finely chopped sweet pickle
½ cup	diced cooked ham
1	hard cooked egg, chopped (p. 105)
1 tbsp.	light mayonnaise
1 tsp.	milk
¼ tsp.	Dijon mustard
	Lettuce

Preparation:
15 minutes
plus chilling

Combine peas, celery, green pepper, onion, and pickle in a bowl and toss lightly. Chill.

Add ham and egg at serving time. Combine mayonnaise, milk, and mustard and pour over salad, then toss lightly. Serve immediately on lettuce. This is a nice big salad suitable for a whole meal.

FAR EAST CHICKEN SALAD
▼▼▼

⅛ tsp.	dry mustard
⅛ tsp.	salt
	Dash Tabasco sauce
½ tsp.	soya sauce
1 tbsp.	salad oil
½ tsp.	lemon juice
¾ cup	slivered cooked chicken
½ cup	very finely shredded iceberg lettuce
¼ cup	match-like strips cucumber
¼ cup	match-like strips raw carrot
1	green onion, cut into 1-inch long strips
¼ cup	bean sprouts
3 tbsp.	slivered toasted almonds
2 tsp.	toasted sesame seeds

Preparation:
15 minutes
plus chilling

Whisk mustard, salt, Tabasco, soya sauce, salad oil, and lemon juice together to blend. Chill.

Combine remaining ingredients except sesame seeds in a shallow bowl and toss with the chilled dressing. Sprinkle with sesame seeds. It's a whole meal!

CHICKEN SALAD WITH GRAPES
▼▼▼

½ cup   cubed cooked
        chicken
¼ cup   diced celery
¼ cup   halved seedless
        green grapes
1 tbsp. chopped green
        pepper
1 tbsp. chopped toasted
        almonds
        Lime Dressing (p. 201)
        Lettuce
        Cantaloupe wedges

Preparation:
10 minutes
plus chilling

Combine chicken, celery, grapes, green pepper, and almonds in a bowl. Add enough Lime Dressing to moisten. Chill.

Cover serving plate with lettuce at serving time, add 2 thin wedges of cantaloupe to outer edge of plate and pile the chicken mixture in the center.

WHOLE MEAL LAYERED SALAD
▼▼▼

¾ cup	shredded iceberg lettuce
½ cup	shredded fresh spinach (see note)
2	large radishes, sliced paper thin
½ cup	cubed cooked chicken
2 tbsp.	sliced celery
2 tbsp.	grated cheddar cheese
3 tbsp.	mayonnaise
⅛ tsp.	Worcestershire sauce
⅛ tsp.	dry mustard
1 tbsp.	sliced green onion

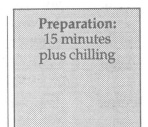

Preparation:
15 minutes
plus chilling

Layer half of each of the first 6 ingredients in a bowl, then repeat layers.

Combine remaining ingredients, except onion, and spread on top of salad. Cover and chill several hours or overnight. Add onion and toss, then serve.

Note: To shred spinach easily, roll up leaves and slice across the roll.

SUPPER SALAD
▼▼▼

1 cup	flaked cooked haddock (or other white fish)
¼ cup	cooked fresh or frozen peas
1 tbsp.	olive oil
1 tsp.	white vinegar
1 tsp.	lemon juice
1 tsp.	chopped fresh mint
	Dash each salt and pepper
	Lettuce

Put fish and peas in a bowl. Shake all remaining ingredients except lettuce in a small jar with a tight lid. Pour over fish mixture and toss lightly. Cover tightly and chill several hours. Pile on lettuce to serve.

TUNA WALDORF SALAD
▼▼▼

1	can (3.75 oz. or 106 g size) tuna, drained
1	small red unpeeled apple, diced
¼ cup	diced celery
2 tbsp.	seedless raisins, plumped in hot water and drained
2 tbsp.	coarsely broken walnuts
1 tbsp.	lemon juice
	Dash each salt and pepper
2 tbsp. (approx.)	light mayonnaise
	Lettuce

Preparation: 10 minutes plus chilling

Break tuna into a bowl, then add all remaining ingredients except lettuce, using just enough of the mayonnaise to moisten. Chill. Pile on lettuce to serve.

SMOKED SALMON SALAD
▼▼▼

½ cup	diced smoked salmon *or* 1 can (3.75 oz. or 106 g size) smoke-flavored salmon, drained and broken up
1 tbsp.	minced green onion
1 tsp.	minced capers
¾ cup	diced cooked potatoes
¼ cup	chopped celery
1 tbsp.	olive oil
1 tsp.	white vinegar
¼ tsp.	Dijon mustard
	Grating fresh pepper
	Lettuce
	Snipped fresh dill

Preparation:
10 minutes
plus chilling

Combine salmon, green onion, capers, potatoes, and celery in a bowl. Blend oil, vinegar, mustard, and pepper and drizzle over, then toss lightly. Chill. Spoon onto lettuce at serving time and sprinkle generously with dill.

191

CRAB-RICE SALAD
▼▼▼

½ cup	cold cooked rice (p. 168)
¼ tsp.	curry powder
2 tbsp.	chopped parsley
2 tsp.	commercial French dressing
2 tbsp.	slivered ripe olives
2 tbsp.	chopped celery
½	can (4.5 oz. or 128 g size) crab, drained
1 tbsp.	mayonnaise
½	small avocado (optional)
	Lime juice
	Lettuce

Preparation:
15 minutes
plus chilling

Combine rice, curry powder, parsley, and French dressing in a bowl and toss lightly. Fold in olives, celery, crab, and mayonnaise. Chill until serving time.

Rub cut surfaces of both halves of avocado with lime juice. Wrap the one you are not using now tightly in transparent wrap and refrigerate for another meal. Peel the second half avocado and cut into four strips lengthwise. Lay these strips on opposite sides of lettuce-lined plate and pile the rice mixture in the middle. This is a whole meal for one. If you have company, it will make a nice side salad for two.

MACARONI-SHRIMP SALAD
▼▼▼

¼ cup	small macaroni shells, cooked
1 cup	small cooked shrimp (see note)
3 tbsp.	chopped celery
1 tbsp.	sliced stuffed olives
1 tsp.	chopped parsley
1½ tbsp.	mayonnaise
2 tsp.	wine vinegar
½ tsp.	lemon juice
	Dash garlic salt
	Pinch dry mustard
	Dash paprika
	Lettuce

Preparation:
15 minutes
plus chilling

Combine macaroni, shrimp, celery, olives, and parsley in a bowl and toss lightly. Combine all remaining ingredients, except lettuce, and add to shrimp mixture, tossing lightly again. Cover tightly and chill well. Serve on lettuce.

Note: You may use fresh cooked, frozen, or canned shrimp. If you used canned, rinse well under cold water.

ORANGE SALAD
▼▼▼

1	small orange, peeled and sectioned
½	small onion, sliced paper thin and separated into rings
1 tbsp.	thin, 1-inch strips pimento
1 cup	torn-up salad greens
1 tbsp.	olive oil
	Salt and pepper
1½ tsp.	wine vinegar

Preparation:
10 minutes

Drain orange sections and put in small salad bowl with onion rings, pimento, and salad greens. Drizzle with the olive oil and toss lightly. Sprinkle lightly with salt and pepper, then add vinegar and toss again. Serve immediately.

Note: Tarragon French Dressing (p. 200) is good with this salad too. Just omit oil and vinegar and use a little of the dressing.

CONFETTI SALAD

¾ cup	cantaloupe cubes
¾ cup	watermelon cubes
¼ cup	halved strawberries
	Leaf lettuce
	Poppy Seed Dressing (p. 202)
	Mint sprigs

Preparation:
10 minutes
plus chilling

Combine fruit and chill well. At serving time, line serving plate with lettuce and top with melon mixture. Add a little of the Poppy Seed Dressing and garnish with mint sprigs.

BUTTERMILK DRESSING
▼▼▼

½ cup	buttermilk
¼ cup	skim milk powder
2 tbsp.	lemon juice
1 tsp.	snipped fresh dill
2	large sprigs parsley
¼ tsp.	salt
	Grating fresh pepper
½	medium cucumber, peeled, seeded, and cut up

Preparation:
7 minutes

Combine all ingredients in a blender and blend until smooth and creamy.

This is good with tomato salads and any combination of greens.

Makes 1 cup.

CARAWAY DRESSING (for coleslaw)
▼▼▼

¼ cup	water
3 tbsp.	white vinegar
1 tbsp.	sugar
¼ tsp.	salt
	Grating fresh pepper
1	egg, beaten
½ tsp.	caraway seeds

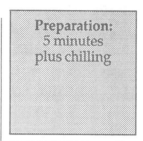

Preparation:
5 minutes
plus chilling

Stir ingredients in a small saucepan over medium heat until slightly thickened. Pour over shredded cabbage while hot, then chill.

Makes about ⅔ cup — enough to dress 5 cups cabbage.

197

CHEESE DRESSING
▼▼▼

2 tbsp.	wine vinegar
	Dash salt
	Grating fresh pepper
⅓ cup	olive oil
2 tsp.	finely chopped watercress leaves
3 tbsp.	finely grated old cheddar cheese
¼ tsp.	Dijon mustard

Preparation:
5 minutes

Beat vinegar, salt, pepper, and oil with a fork or a wire whip until thickened and blended. Add remaining ingredients and beat again until creamy. Good on lettuce wedge or any greens.

Makes ½ cup.

DIETER'S DRESSING
▼▼▼

½ cup	cold water
2 tsp.	cornstarch
¼ tsp.	dry mustard
⅓ cup	wine vinegar
2 tbsp.	lemon juice
1 tbsp.	chopped parsley
½ tsp.	dried leaf basil
¼ tsp.	paprika
	Dash salt
	Grating fresh pepper

Preparation:
7 minutes
plus chilling

Combine cold water, cornstarch, and mustard in a small saucepan, blending well. Stir in vinegar and lemon juice, set over high heat and stir until boiling and slightly thickened. Reduce heat and simmer, stirring, 3 minutes. Stir in remaining ingredients and chill until needed.

Makes about 1 cup.

FRENCH DRESSING
▼▼▼

½ cup	olive oil
2 tbsp.	wine vinegar
2 tbsp.	lemon juice
¼ tsp.	salt
¼ tsp.	dry mustard
¼ tsp.	paprika

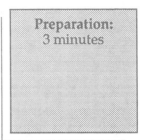

Preparation:
3 minutes

Shake all ingredients together in a small jar with a tight lid. Keep in refrigerator. Shake again before using.

Makes ¾ cup.

VARIATIONS

Garlic French Dressing

Add 1 medium clove garlic, crushed, to French Dressing.

Tarragon French Dressing

Add ⅛ tsp. dried leaf tarragon or ¼ tsp. snipped fresh tarragon to French Dressing.

Italian Dressing

Make Garlic French Dressing, increasing mustard to ½ tsp. and adding ½ tsp. each sugar, dried leaf basil, and dried leaf oregano and a good grating of fresh pepper.

LIME DRESSING
▼▼▼

½ cup	light mayonnaise
⅛ tsp.	curry powder
¼ tsp.	grated lime rind
1½ tsp.	lime juice
1	egg yolk, beaten

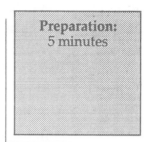

Preparation:
5 minutes

Combine mayonnaise, curry powder, lime rind, and juice in a small saucepan. Add egg yolk and stir over medium-low heat until mixture is smooth, blended, and warm but not boiling, about 3 minutes. Cool. Especially good on chicken and fruit salads.

Makes ½ cup.

POPPY SEED DRESSING

¼ cup	salad oil
1½ tbsp.	orange juice
1 tbsp.	liquid honey
	Pinch salt
⅛ tsp.	dry mustard
⅛ tsp.	paprika
1 tsp.	poppy seeds

Preparation:
5 minutes

Combine all ingredients in a small jar with a tight lid and shake to blend well. Good with any fruit salad.

Makes about ⅓ cup.

SOYA DRESSING
▼▼▼

1 tsp.	unflavored gelatin
½ cup	tomato juice
2 tbsp.	soya sauce
1 tbsp.	lemon juice
1 tbsp.	wine vinegar
1 tbsp.	water
2 tsp.	Dijon mustard
¼ tsp.	dried leaf chervil
2 tbsp.	chopped parsley

Preparation:
15 minutes
plus chilling

Combine gelatin and tomato juice in a small dish and let stand 5 minutes. Set in a pan of simmering water and heat until gelatin dissolves. Cool but do not chill. Combine all ingredients in a small jar with a tight lid and shake to blend well. Chill. Shake again before using with any mixture of greens. This is a full-flavored, yet low-calorie dressing.

Makes ¾ cup.

SWEET-SOUR SALAD DRESSING
▼▼▼

½ cup	olive oil
3 tbsp.	wine vinegar
2 tbsp.	chili sauce
1½ tbsp.	mayonnaise
1 tbsp.	sugar
½ tsp.	paprika
	Dash salt
	Dash Tabasco sauce
½	small clove garlic, minced (optional)

Preparation:
5 minutes

Combine all ingredients in a small jar with a tight lid and shake to blend well. Store in refrigerator and shake again before using. Good with a simple lettuce salad or with a more glamorous seafood salad.

Makes about ¾ cup.

YOGURT DRESSING
▼▼▼

½ cup	plain low-fat yogurt
1½ tbsp.	chili sauce
1½ tsp.	finely chopped green pepper
1 tsp.	finely chopped pimento
½ tsp.	chopped chives

Preparation:
7 minutes
plus chilling

Drain yogurt in a sieve for a few minutes to get rid of excess liquid. Blend drained yogurt with all remaining ingredients and chill. Good on lettuce wedges or any green salad.

Makes ⅔ cup.

ZESTY DRESSING
▼▼▼

¼ cup	olive oil
1 tbsp.	sugar
1½ tbsp.	ketchup
1 tbsp.	white vinegar
¾ tsp.	Worcestershire sauce
¾ tsp.	grated onion

Preparation:
5 minutes
plus chilling

Combine all ingredients in a small jar with a tight lid and shake to blend well. Chill, then shake again before using.

Makes about ½ cup.

BREAD & SANDWICHES

▼▼▼

BREAD AND SANDWICHES
▼▼▼

Recipes for quick breads are handy. If you have the ingredients you can whip up some muffins in a hurry for unexpected company. Or you can pull a loaf of special bread out of the freezer and thaw and heat it in the microwave. Add some butter and maybe some cheese or jelly and you have something you can be proud to serve with a cup of tea or coffee — or are glad to have for a treat for yourself. A couple of muffin recipes and a quick-to-make loaf are here.

Most of us who are alone have sandwiches fairly often. One of my favorites is *warm* hard-cooked eggs, chopped and mixed with celery, green or red pepper, green onions, and a touch of light mayonnaise. That, spread in a warm pita or between slices of whole wheat toast is *very* good. However, many other sandwiches are wonderfully tasty too and you'll find quite a selection here.

RICH CORNMEAL MUFFINS

1	egg
½ cup	milk
3 tbsp.	melted butter or margarine
¼ cup	sugar
½ cup	cornmeal
¾ cup	sifted all-purpose flour
2 tsp.	baking powder
¼ tsp.	salt

Preparation:
5 minutes
Baking:
15 minutes

Heat oven to 400 °F. Grease 6 large muffin cups.

Beat egg in medium mixing bowl. Stir in milk, melted butter or margarine, sugar, and cornmeal. Sift flour, baking powder, and salt together and add, stirring just to blend. Spoon into muffin cups, filling about ⅔ full. Bake about 15 minutes. Serve warm.

Makes 6 large.

OATMEAL-DATE MUFFINS
▼▼▼

1	egg
¾ cup	milk
¾ cup	quick-cooking rolled oats
½ cup	whole wheat flour
¼ cup	packed brown sugar
2 tbsp.	cooking oil
½ cup	chopped dates
½ cup	all-purpose flour
2 tsp.	baking powder
¼ tsp.	salt

Preparation: 10 minutes
Baking: 15 minutes

Heat oven to 400 °F. Grease 8 large muffin cups.

Beat egg and milk together in a medium bowl. Add rolled oats and let stand 5 minutes. Stir in whole wheat flour, sugar, oil, and dates.

Sift all-purpose flour, baking powder, and salt together into mixture and stir just to blend. Batter should be a little lumpy.

Spoon into muffin cups, filling about ⅔ full. Bake about 15 minutes.

Makes 8.

APPLE BREAD
▼▼▼

¼ cup	soft butter or margarine
⅔ cup	sugar
2	eggs
¼ cup	milk
1½ cups	grated peeled apples (medium grater)
½ cup	seedless raisins
2 cups	whole wheat flour
1 tsp.	baking powder
½ tsp.	baking soda
½ tsp.	ground cinnamon
¼ tsp.	salt

Preparation:
10 minutes
Baking:
about 50 minutes

Heat oven to 350°F. Grease 2 small foil loaf pans, 5½ x 3¼ x 2 inches.

Beat butter or margarine, sugar, eggs, and milk together well. Stir in grated apple and raisins.

Stir remaining ingredients together with a fork and add to first mixture, stirring just until blended.

Turn into prepared pans and bake about 50 minutes or until a toothpick stuck in the center comes out clean. Can be frozen.

Makes 2 small loaves.

GARLIC BREAD
▼▼▼

¼ cup	soft butter or margarine
1	small clove garlic, crushed
1 tbsp.	finely chopped parsley
3 drops	lemon juice
	Dash each pepper and seasoned salt
½	small loaf French bread or 1 long crusty roll

Preparation:
5 minutes
Heating:
15 minutes

Combine all ingredients except bread or roll. Slice bread or roll quite thick and spread garlicky mixture generously between slices. Wrap in heavy foil.

Near serving time, heat oven to 400 °F. Heat bread 15 minutes or until very hot and crusty. Loosen foil immediately to let steam escape and eat hot.

HAM AND CHEESE SPREAD

½ cup	finely ground leftover cooked ham
¾ cup	grated old cheddar cheese
1 tbsp.	minced onion
1 tsp.	prepared mustard
½ tsp.	Worcestershire sauce
⅛ tsp.	chili powder
3 tbsp.	light mayonnaise

Preparation:
5 minutes

Combine all ingredients and refrigerate until needed. It will keep in the refrigerator for several days.

Makes about 1 cup — enough for 4 sandwiches.

GRILLED BREAKFAST SANDWICH
▼▼▼

2 slices	bacon
1 tbsp.	thinly sliced green onion
1	hard-cooked egg, chopped (p. 105)
¼ cup	grated Swiss cheese
1 tbsp.	mayonnaise
½ tsp.	Dijon mustard
2 slices	whole wheat bread
	Soft butter or margarine

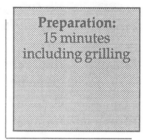

Preparation:
15 minutes
including grilling

Fry bacon until crisp. Drain, cool, and crumble, then combine with onion, hard-cooked egg, cheese, mayonnaise, and mustard. Spread between the slices of bread.

Spread one side of the sandwich with butter or margarine and put it, buttered side down, in a hot heavy skillet over medium heat. Grill until brown, then butter second side, turn, and brown. Serve hot.

COTTAGE CHEESE SANDWICH
▼▼▼

⅓ cup	1% cottage cheese
2 tbsp.	finely grated carrot
1 tbsp.	finely chopped green pepper
1 tsp.	chopped pimento
1 tsp.	finely chopped green onion
	Dash each salt and pepper
	Soft butter or margarine
1	large slice rye bread
	Lettuce
1	large thick slice tomato

Preparation:
10 minutes
plus chilling

Combine cottage cheese, carrot, green pepper, pimento, green onion, salt, and pepper, mixing well with a fork. Chill.

Butter bread at serving time. Top with lettuce, then with tomato slice. Add cottage cheese mixture and eat immediately with a knife and fork.

CHICKEN PITA POCKETS
▼▼▼

1½ tbsp.	mayonnaise
1 tsp.	ketchup
⅛ tsp.	grated onion
1 tsp.	finely chopped green pepper
½ tsp.	finely chopped stuffed olives
	Butter or margarine
1	small pita bread, heated and cut in half
2	thin slices chicken breast
2	slices Swiss cheese
4	thin slices tomato
	Shredded lettuce

Preparation:
10 minutes
including heating
pita

Combine mayonnaise, ketchup, onion, green pepper, and olives. Spread butter or margarine lightly inside warm pita pieces. Fill each with a slice of chicken, a cheese slice, 2 tomato slices, and some shredded lettuce. Spread with the mayonnaise mixture.

To heat pita bread: Wrap bread in foil and heat 10 minutes in 400°F oven before cutting in half and opening carefully to make pita pockets.

To heat in microwave: Set on paper towelling and heat 1 small pita 30 seconds or 2 small pitas 45 seconds or until warm.

MEXICAN-STYLE PITA POCKETS
▼▼▼

	Soft butter or margarine
2	**small pita breads, heated and cut into halves**
1	**can (3.75 oz. or 106 g size) solid tuna, drained and flaked**
2	**large thin slices Spanish onion, cut in half**
4	**anchovies, chopped**
1	**small hot green pepper, finely chopped**
2 tbsp.	**chopped parsley**
8	**thin slices tomato**
	Fresh basil, chopped (optional)

**Preparation:
10 minutes
including heating
pitas**

Spread butter or margarine lightly inside warm pita pieces. Put a layer of tuna in each, then divide remaining ingredients among them, using only a small sprinkling of hot pepper until you taste — then add more if desired.

Note: See p. 217 for heating pitas.

VEGETABLE PITA POCKETS
▼▼▼

2 tbsp.	mayonnaise
1 tbsp.	finely chopped green pepper
1 tbsp.	finely chopped onion
	Dash each salt and pepper
¼ cup	thinly sliced radishes
½ cup	peeled, seeded, and chopped cucumber
2	small pita breads, heated and cut into halves
	Soft butter or margarine
	Shredded lettuce

Preparation:
10 minutes
including heating
pitas

Combine mayonnaise, green pepper, onion, salt, and pepper. Mix radishes and cucumber. Spread inside of pita pieces lightly with butter or margarine. Divide radish-cucumber mixture and mayonnaise mixture among them. Add some lettuce.

Note: See p. 217 for heating pitas.

PEPPER AND CHEESE SANDWICHES
▼▼▼

1	crusty roll, about 5½ inches long
1 tbsp.	soft butter or margarine
2 tsp.	lightly toasted sesame seeds
½ cup	grated old cheddar cheese
2	thin rings green pepper
2	thin rings red pepper
	Olive oil

Preparation:
5 minutes
Baking:
10 minutes

Split roll lengthwise and put halves, crust side up, on cookie sheet. Toast lightly under the broiler. Remove from oven and turn crust side down. Heat oven to 400 °F.

Combine butter or margarine and sesame seeds and spread on untoasted sides of bun. Top each with a generous amount of grated cheese and a ring each of green and red pepper. Drizzle each with ¼ tsp. olive oil. Bake 10 minutes or until very hot and cheese is bubbling.

HOT ROAST BEEF SANDWICH
▼▼▼

½ cup	**leftover gravy**
½ tsp.	**prepared mustard**
¼ cup	**finely chopped dill pickles**
	Thin slices leftover roast beef
	Toasted French or Italian bread

Preparation:
5 minutes
Cooking:
6 minutes

Combine gravy, mustard, and pickles in a small skillet. Bring to a boil, reduce heat, and simmer 5 minutes. Add beef slices and heat just long enough to be sure beef is hot, about 1 minute. Spoon onto toast on hot serving plate and serve with sliced tomatoes for lunch or supper.

221

FRENCH-TOASTED HAM SANDWICH
▼▼▼

¼ cup	ground leftover cooked ham
1½ tbsp.	grated process cheese
1½ tsp.	chopped ripe olives
½ tsp.	finely chopped green onion
	Dash chili powder
1½ tsp.	mayonnaise
2	slices whole wheat bread
1½ tsp.	butter or margarine
1	egg, lightly beaten
1 tbsp.	milk

Preparation:
10 minutes
Cooking:
10 minutes

Combine ham, cheese, olives, onion, chili powder, and mayonnaise. Spread mixture between the slices of bread.

Heat butter or margarine in small heavy skillet. Beat egg and milk in a flat dish and dip sandwich into mixture to coat both sides. (Don't let sandwich soak in egg.) Fry slowly in hot butter or margarine, adding a little more fat if necessary, until bread is golden and filling is very hot. Easiest to eat with a knife and fork. Good for breakfast or lunch.

SKILLET SALMON SANDWICH
▼▼▼

1	can (3.75 oz. or 106 g size) salmon
1 tbsp.	mayonnaise
1½ tsp.	chopped green onion
1 tsp.	chopped parsley
	Dash each salt and pepper
⅛ tsp.	curry powder
2	slices whole wheat bread, buttered
1½ tsp.	butter or margarine
1	egg

Preparation: 15 minutes including frying time

Drain salmon, saving 1 tbsp. of the liquid in a flat dish or plate. Put salmon, including bones and skin, in a bowl. Mash bones with a fork and break up salmon well. Add mayonnaise, onion, parsley, salt, pepper, and curry powder and blend well. Spread on buttered side of one slice of bread and top with other slice.

Heat butter or margarine in small skillet. Break egg into saved salmon liquid and beat together with a fork. Dip sandwich into egg mixture quickly to coat both sides. Put in skillet and brown slowly on both sides, adding butter or margarine if needed. Serve hot.

OPEN-FACE SALMON SANDWICHES
▼▼▼

½ cup	flaked, canned salmon
1 tbsp.	mayonnaise
1 tbsp.	plain yogurt
½ tsp.	grated onion
⅛ tsp.	snipped fresh dill
1	egg white
	Dash each salt and pepper
	Butter or margarine
2 slices	rye bread, lightly toasted
1 tbsp.	grated Parmesan cheese

Preparation:
7 minutes
including broiling
time

Heat broiler. Combine salmon, mayonnaise, yogurt, onion, and dill. Beat egg white, salt, and pepper until stiff and fold into salmon mixture.

Lightly butter toasted rye bread and spread each slice with some of the salmon mixture. Sprinkle each with half the Parmesan cheese. Put on a cookie sheet and slip low under the broiler (about 6 inches from the heat source). Broil until bubbling and lightly browned and serve hot.

Makes 2.

OPEN-FACE SARDINE SANDWICHES
▼▼▼

2	slices whole wheat bread
1 tbsp.	butter or margarine
½ tsp.	Worcestershire sauce
	Dash Tabasco sauce
8 to 12	sardines
¼ cup	1% cottage cheese
	Paprika

Preparation:
5 minutes

Heat broiler. Put bread on small cookie sheet and toast lightly on both sides under hot broiler.

Blend butter or margarine, Worcestershire sauce, and Tabasco sauce and spread toast with mixture. Lay 2 or 3 sardines along two opposite edges of each slice of bread and pile the cottage cheese down the middle. Slip low under the broiler and broil just to heat slightly. Remove from oven, sprinkle cheese lightly with paprika, and serve warm. Makes 2.

SHRIMP BUNS
▼▼▼

¼ lb.	cooked, shelled, cleaned shrimp
2 tbsp.	tiny cubes Swiss cheese
1½ tsp.	thinly sliced green onion
	Pinch dried dill weed
	Dash each salt and pepper
1½ tsp.	mayonnaise
¼ tsp.	white wine vinegar
2	sesame hamburger buns or soft dinner rolls
	Butter or margarine
2	stuffed olives

Preparation:
10 minutes
Heating:
20 minutes

Choose 2 perfect shrimp and set them aside for garnish. Chop remaining shrimp coarsely and mix with cheese, onion, dill weed, salt, pepper, mayonnaise, and vinegar.

Split buns and butter. Spread bottom halves with shrimp mixture and replace tops. Wrap each in foil and refrigerate until needed. Heat oven to 350 °F when ready to eat. Heat sandwiches 20 minutes. Put the 2 shrimp for garnish and the olives on 2 toothpicks and stick them in the tops of the sandwiches.

Makes 2.

SWEETS

▼▼▼

SWEETS

▼▼▼

Cookies and cake are certainly tasty for dessert and I like and use the ones I have included here. The cake I've chosen is Pound Cake (p. 232). I like to make it because it keeps especially well and can be used in different ways. For example, thin slices are the basis for trifle-like Strawberry Bagatelle (p. 240) or a thick slice, steamed, makes a good cool weather dessert as in Steamed Cake with Raspberry Sauce (p. 233).

But puddings and fruit dishes are no doubt better for us, and usually much easier to prepare.

These recipes using apples, bananas, blueberries, grapes, peaches, pears, strawberries, and raspberries are so wonderfully delightful it's hard to believe they really are (mostly) good for us too.

BUTTER-CHIP COOKIES
▼▼▼

½ cup	soft butter
½ cup	packed brown sugar
¼ cup	granulated sugar
1	egg
2 tbsp.	hot water
½ tsp.	baking soda
1½ cups	whole wheat flour
¼ tsp.	salt
1 cup	chocolate chips
½ cup	chopped walnuts or pecans
½ tsp.	vanilla extract

Preparation:
10 minutes
Baking:
8 to 10 minutes

Heat oven to 375 °F. Grease cookie sheets.

Beat butter, brown sugar, sugar, and egg together well. Measure hot water into a small dish and add soda. Mix flour and salt with a fork. Stir flour into butter mixture alternately with water-soda mixture. Blend in chocolate chips, nuts, and vanilla.

Drop by rounded teaspoonfuls on prepared cookie sheets. Bake just above the middle of the oven 8 to 10 minutes or until browned.

Makes about 4 dozen.

ORANGE OATMEAL COOKIES
▼▼▼

½ cup	soft shortening or margarine
1 cup	packed brown sugar
1	egg
1 tbsp.	grated orange rind
2 tbsp.	orange juice
1 cup	quick-cooking rolled oats
½ cup	seedless raisins
1 cup	sifted all-purpose flour
½ tsp.	baking soda
	Dash salt

Preparation:
10 minutes
Baking:
10 to 12 minutes

Heat oven to 350 °F. Grease cookie sheets.

Beat shortening or margarine, sugar, and egg until fluffy. Beat in orange rind and juice. Stir in rolled oats and raisins. Sift flour, soda, and salt into mixture and stir to blend.

Drop by rounded teaspoonfuls 2 inches apart on cookie sheets. Bake just above the middle of the oven 10 to 12 minutes.

Makes 3 dozen.

POUND CAKE
▼▼▼

⅔ cup	**soft butter**
⅔ cup	**sugar**
2	**eggs**
2 tsp.	**water**
½ tsp.	**lemon extract**
1⅓ cups	**sifted all-purpose flour**
¼ tsp.	**baking powder**

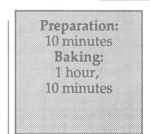

Preparation:
10 minutes
Baking:
1 hour,
10 minutes

Heat oven to 275°F. Grease a foil loaf pan, 7½ x 3½ x 2 inches. (If you are using a metal pan, line with greased heavy brown paper.)

Cream butter until fluffy. Add sugar gradually, creaming well after each addition. Add eggs one at a time and beat well after each. Beat in water and lemon extract. Sift in dry ingredients and stir just to blend. Turn into prepared pan and bake about 1 hour and 10 minutes, or until a toothpick stuck in the center comes out clean. Cool in pan 5 minutes then turn out on rack to finish cooling.

STEAMED CAKE (with Raspberry Sauce)
▼▼▼

1   slice Pound cake
          (p. 232)

Preparation:
3 minutes
Steaming:
15 minutes

Use thick slice of Pound Cake or baker's cake. Put the cake in a sieve over simmering water, cover, and steam 15 minutes or until cake is very hot. Heat some of the Raspberry Sauce (p. 243). Put cake in serving dish and spoon hot sauce over.

CODDLED APPLE
▼▼▼

1	large cooking apple
1 tbsp.	water
1½ tbsp.	brown sugar
¼ tsp.	grated lemon rind
⅛ tsp.	ground cinnamon
1 tbsp.	red currant jelly
2	drops vanilla extract
2 tbsp.	plain yogurt
	Brown sugar (optional)

Preparation:
7 minutes
Cooking:
10 minutes
plus chilling

Peel and slice apple into a small saucepan. Add water, 1½ tbsp. brown sugar, lemon rind, and cinnamon and bring to a boil over medium heat. Reduce heat, cover, and simmer until apple is just beginning to get tender, about 5 minutes. Add jelly, cover again, and simmer until apple is tender and jelly is melted, about 3 minutes. (Cooking time depends on kind of apple used.) Remove from heat, add vanilla, and stir carefully so as not to break up apple slices. Cover and chill.

Put 1 tbsp. yogurt in the bottom of a sherbet glass at serving time. Add the apple slices and top with remaining yogurt. Sprinkle lightly with brown sugar.

BLUEBERRIES AND BANANA CREAM
▼▼▼

½ cup	fresh blueberries
2 tbsp.	plain yogurt
1 tsp.	brown sugar
¼ tsp.	lemon juice
¼ tsp.	vanilla extract
1	small banana

Preparation:
7 minutes

Wash blueberries and put in a large sherbet glass. Combine yogurt, brown sugar, lemon juice, and vanilla. Peel banana, mash with a fork until quite well broken up and add to yogurt. Pour over berries.

MINTED GRAPES
▼▼▼

1 cup	**halved seedless green grapes**
1 tbsp.	**liquid honey**
2 tsp.	**lime juice**
2 tsp.	**finely chopped fresh mint leaves**
	Sour cream or plain yogurt
	Sprig mint

Preparation:
10 minutes
plus chilling

Combine grapes, honey, lime juice, and chopped mint. Cover and chill several hours. Spoon into sherbet glass and top with a dab of sour cream or yogurt. Garnish with a mint sprig.

NUTMEG SPICED PEACH

2	canned peach halves
1 tbsp.	juice from peaches
2 tsp.	butter
1 tsp.	brown sugar
⅛ tsp.	ground nutmeg
	Vanilla ice cream
	or lemon sherbet

Preparation:
10 minutes

Drain peach halves. Combine peach juice, butter, sugar, and nutmeg in a small saucepan and heat to boiling. Add peach halves and simmer 5 minutes, turning occasionally, until hot and glazed. Put a scoop of ice cream or sherbet in a large sherbet glass or goblet and spoon on the hot peach halves and liquid.

PEAR WITH LIQUEUR
▼▼▼

1	pear, peeled, cored, and sliced thin
1 tbsp.	orange liqueur (Curaçao or Cointreau)
2 tbsp.	orange juice
1 tsp.	grated orange rind

Preparation:
5 minutes
plus chilling

Put sliced pear into a serving dish or large sherbet glass. Drizzle with the liqueur and orange juice. Cover and chill well. Sprinkle with orange rind at serving time.

SHERRIED PEAR
▼▼▼

1	large pear
¼ cup	sweet sherry
2 tbsp.	slivered almonds
1 tsp.	liquid honey
⅛ tsp.	almond extract

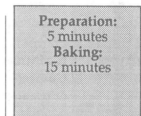

Preparation:
5 minutes
Baking:
15 minutes

Heat oven to 350°F. Peel, cut in half, and core pear. Put in a small baking dish just large enough to hold the halves, cut side up. Pour sherry over them and put almonds, honey, and almond extract in the cavities.

Bake, uncovered, basting often until pear is tender, about 15 minutes. Serve hot or cold with ice cream if desired.

STRAWBERRY BAGATELLE
▼▼▼

1 cup	sliced fresh strawberries
1 tbsp.	orange liqueur (Cointreau or Curaçao) or orange juice
8	small thin slices Pound Cake (p. 232)
½ cup	vanilla yogurt (see note)
	Sliced strawberries
1 tbsp.	toasted slivered almonds (optional)

Preparation:
10 to 15 minutes
plus chilling

Combine 1 cup sliced strawberries and orange liqueur or orange juice in the blender and blend until berries are broken up but not smooth. (If you don't have a blender, mash berries with a fork.) Put 1 slice of cake in each of 2 custard cups, spread each with ¼ of the crushed berries. Add a second layer of cake and spread each with ¼ of the yogurt. Repeat layers. Cover and chill well.

Garnish top of dessert with sliced strawberries and almonds at serving time. This dessert, like trifle, improves on standing. It makes 2 small desserts and you'll find it very good even if it stands 2 or 3 days.

Note: You can replace the vanilla yogurt with your own mixture. Drain ½ cup low-fat yogurt and stir in 1 tsp. sugar and ¼ tsp. vanilla extract.

APPLE CRISP
▼▼▼

2	cooking apples (e.g., McIntosh, Spy, Spartan)
2 tbsp.	water
¼ tsp.	ground cinnamon
	Dash salt
3 tbsp.	soft butter
¼ cup	brown sugar
⅓ cup	whole wheat flour
	Vanilla ice cream

Preparation:
10 minutes
Baking:
30 minutes

Heat oven to 350 °F. Butter a small casserole, 2 cup size.

Peel and slice apples into casserole, sprinkle with water, cinnamon, and salt. Blend remaining ingredients, except ice cream, with a fork and then with fingers to make a crumbly mixture. Sprinkle over apples and pat down lightly.

Bake about 30 minutes (time depends on the kind of apples) or until apples are tender. Serve topped with ice cream. Good both hot and cold.

Makes 2 servings.

PEACH PUDDING
▼▼▼

1	ripe medium peach, peeled and sliced thick
1	egg
½ cup	sugar
¼ tsp.	ground cinnamon
1½ cups	¼-inch soft bread cubes
1 tbsp.	melted butter
	Butterscotch Sauce (p. 244)

Preparation:
10 minutes
Baking:
20 minutes

Heat oven to 400 °F. Lightly butter a small casserole, 2 cup size.

Put peach slices in prepared casserole. Beat egg, adding sugar gradually and beating well after each addition. Stir in cinnamon, bread cubes, and butter. Spoon over peach pieces.

Bake about 20 minutes or until topping is set and browned. Serve warm or cold with warm Butterscotch Sauce.

Makes 2 servings.

RASPBERRY SAUCE
▼▼▼

½	pkg. (300 g or about 10 oz. size) unsweetened frozen raspberries (or 1 cup fresh)
¼ cup	water
2 tbsp.	sugar
2 tsp.	cornstarch
2 tsp.	grated orange rind

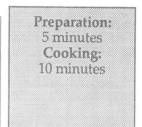

Preparation:
5 minutes
Cooking:
10 minutes

Combine berries and water in a small saucepan, cover, and bring to a boil over medium heat. Boil until berries are broken up, then put through a sieve to remove seeds. Measure purée and add water to make ½ cup if necessary. Bring raspberry purée to a boil. Mix sugar and cornstarch thoroughly and stir into boiling liquid very gradually, stirring briskly all the time. Mixture should be thick and clear when all the sugar mixture is added. Reduce heat to low and simmer 2 minutes, then stir in orange rind. Serve hot or cold. If you are serving cold you may want to thin the sauce a little, using orange juice or orange liqueur. Sauce will keep in refrigerator at least a week.

Makes about ½ cup.

BUTTERSCOTCH SAUCE
▼▼▼

1 tbsp.	**cornstarch**
⅓ cup	**packed brown sugar**
⅓ cup	**cold water**
⅓ cup	**boiling water**
1 tbsp.	**butter**
½ tsp.	**vanilla extract**

Preparation:
3 minutes
Cooking:
2 minutes

Mix cornstarch and sugar thoroughly in a small saucepan. Stir in cold water, blending until smooth. Stir in boiling water. Bring to a boil over high heat, stirring constantly. Reduce heat and boil 1 minute. Remove from heat and stir in butter and vanilla. Serve hot.

Makes about ⅔ cup.

SNACKS, SIPS & SAUCES

▼▼▼

SNACKS, SIPS, AND SAUCES
▼▼▼

Being alone is no reason not to have a little snack as an appetizer before dinner. I know I enjoy a cracker and cheese or a spread or dip along with a drink (usually not alcoholic) while I watch the evening news. So here are recipes for a few dips and spreads in smallish amounts as well as a tasty Tuna Pâté (p. 250) that is pleasant to serve to company along with a glass of wine.

As for drinks, there are sips of various kinds, mostly fruit based. And I've added a few odds and ends, too — a Ham Glaze (p. 256), and my favorite Sweet-Hot Mustard (p. 256), and some sauces you'll find useful.

GUACAMOLE
▼▼▼

	Salt
1	**small clove garlic, cut in half**
½	**large avocado**
⅛ tsp.	**chili powder**
½ tsp.	**lemon juice**
1 tsp.	**finely chopped onion**
	Mayonnaise
	Sesame crackers or corn chips

Preparation:
5 minutes
plus
chilling time

Sprinkle a little salt in a small bowl and rub bowl all over with cut sides of garlic. Discard garlic. Mash avocado in bowl with a fork. Stir in chili powder, lemon juice, and onion. Put in a small serving dish and cover top completely with a thin coating of mayonnaise (this will keep avocado from darkening). Cover and chill.

Stir in mayonnaise at serving time and serve as a spread or dip with sesame crackers or corn chips.

EGGPLANT APPETIZER
▼▼▼

1	small eggplant (about ½ lb.)
1½ tsp.	olive oil
¼ cup	finely chopped onion
¼ cup	finely chopped green pepper
2 tbsp.	flaked coconut
	Dash Tabasco sauce
1 tbsp.	lemon juice
	Dash salt

Preparation:
50 minutes
including
baking eggplant
Chilling:
several hours

Heat oven to 400°F. Oil a pie plate.

Wash eggplant and prick in a few places with a fork. Put on the pie plate and bake 30 to 40 minutes or until soft. Cool and peel. Slice, then chop pieces very finely and put in a bowl.

Heat oil in small skillet and add onion and green pepper. Cook gently until limp but not brown, about 5 minutes. Add to eggplant, then mix in coconut, Tabasco sauce, lemon juice, and salt. Cover and chill several hours. Taste and add salt if needed. Serve as a spread on crackers.

TUNA PÂTÉ
▼▼▼

1½ tsp.	unflavored gelatin
2 tbsp.	cold water
1 tbsp.	dry sherry
1	can (3.75 oz. or 106 g size) tuna
1½ tsp.	lemon juice
¼ tsp.	seasoned salt
	Pinch dried dill weed
	Dash Tabasco sauce
1	pkg. (125 g or about 4 oz.) cream cheese, room temperature
⅛ tsp.	unflavored gelatin (optional)
2 tbsp.	canned tomato sauce (optional)
⅛ tsp.	chicken stock mix (optional)
	Melba toast or crackers

Preparation:
10 minutes
plus chilling for
tuna mixture
10 minutes
plus chilling
for glaze

Add 1½ tsp. gelatin to cold water and let stand 5 minutes. Set in a pan of simmering water and heat until gelatin dissolves. Remove from heat and stir in sherry. Drain and flake tuna. Combine with lemon juice, seasoned salt, dill, Tabasco, and gelatin mixture in blender and blend until smooth. Add cheese, a small piece at a time, and blend after each addition. Oil a small bowl and press mixture into it. Chill several hours. Turn out on serving plate.

Add ⅛ tsp. gelatin to tomato sauce and let stand 5 minutes. Add stock mix, set in pan of simmering water, and heat until gelatin dissolves. Chill until slightly thickened, then pour over tuna pâté. Chill until set. Serve with melba toast or crackers.

CHEESE-STUFFED EGGS

2	hard cooked eggs (p. 105)
1 tbsp.	soft butter or margarine
1 tbsp.	grated Swiss cheese
¼ tsp.	prepared hot mustard
	Paprika

Preparation:
5 minutes
plus
chilling time

Cut eggs in half lengthwise and carefully lift out yolks, putting them into a bowl. Mash yolks with a fork, then add butter or margarine, cheese, and mustard and mix well. Spoon back into egg whites, piling high. Sprinkle with paprika and chill. Serve as salad or hors d'oeuvres.

STRAWBERRY-ORANGE FRAPPÉ
▼▼▼

1 cup	fresh strawberries
½ cup	fresh orange juice
4	ice cubes

Preparation:
5 minutes

Combine ingredients in the blender and blend until fruit is puréed and ice is broken into small pieces. Serve in champagne glass.

Makes 2 servings.

VARIATIONS USING ORANGE JUICE

Cranberry Pickup

Combine ½ cup cranberry juice cocktail and ½ cup fresh orange juice and chill well. Serve over ice in a goblet.

Orange Juice and Wine

Half fill a tall glass with fresh orange juice. Add chilled dry white wine to within 1½ inches of the top of the glass, then add an ice cube and top off with soda water.

LIMEADE
▼▼▼

½ cup	sugar
½ cup	boiling water
¼ cup	packed chopped fresh mint leaves
½ cup	lime juice
2 tbsp.	lemon juice
3 cups	water
	Ice cubes
	Mint sprigs

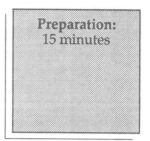

Preparation:
15 minutes

Combine sugar, boiling water and mint. Stir until sugar dissolves, then let steep 10 minutes. Strain and cool.

Put mint syrup in a jar and stir in lime juice, lemon juice, and water. Cover tightly and chill well.

Pour over ice cubes in a tall glass to serve. Will keep in refrigerator several days.

Makes 4 glasses.

HOT TOMATO JUICE

1 cup	tomato juice
1	bunch celery leaves
¼ tsp.	beef stock mix
1	small piece bay leaf
¼ tsp.	grated onion
	Pinch celery salt
	Pinch sugar
	Dash Tabasco sauce
1 tsp.	minced parsley
1 tsp.	lemon juice
1	thin slice lemon

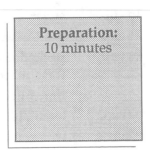

Preparation:
10 minutes

Combine all ingredients except parsley, lemon juice, and lemon slice in a small saucepan. Bring to a boil, reduce heat, and simmer 5 minutes, then strain into a heated mug. Stir in parsley and lemon juice and float the lemon slice on top.

VARIATION

Icy Tomato Juice

1 cup	tomato juice
½ tsp.	Worcestershire sauce
	Dash Tabasco sauce
¼ tsp.	onion juice
	Dash celery salt

Combine all ingredients and freeze half in a small dish. Chill remaining juice. Remove frozen mixture from freezer 30 minutes before serving. At serving time chop frozen juice coarsely and put in a short glass. Pour in remaining juice. Stir and garnish with a dill sprig.

CRÈME FRAÎCHE
▼▼▼

½ cup   commercial
sour cream

½ cup   whipping cream
(see note)

Preparation:
3 minutes
Standing:
(room temp.):
8 to 12 hours
Chilling:
24 hours

Put sour cream in a small bowl. With an electric mixer at low speed, gradually mix in the whipping cream, beating only until smooth. Pour into a jar with a wide mouth and a tight fitting lid. Cover and let stand at room temperature until very thick, 8 to 12 hours. (You can start after dinner and it will be thickened by morning.)

Stir lightly with a fork, cover again and refrigerate at least 24 hours before using.

Makes 1 cup.

Note: This can be used in such dishes as Pork Normande (p. 44) and Baked Scallops (p. 98). It is also delicious over fruit or other desserts where sour cream or whipped cream might be used. Its slightly nutty flavor also enriches soups and, in small amounts, gives a special velvety texture to sauces. It can be boiled without curdling and will keep in the refrigerator 10 to 14 days. I have also made it with light cream in place of the whipping cream and find that it thickens satisfactorily.

SPICY HAM GLAZE
▼▼▼

¼ cup	liquid honey
2 tbsp.	port wine
⅛ tsp.	ground cinnamon
8	whole cloves
	Prepared mustard

Preparation:
3 minutes

This glaze is suitable for a piece of regular ham, a cottage roll, or a piece of back bacon. Cook the meat until about 20 minutes before it is done. Put it in a roasting pan if necessary.

Mix honey, wine, and cinnamon. Stud meat with cloves and spread lightly with mustard. Put in 425°F oven and bake for about 20 minutes, basting often.

Sweet-Hot Mustard

Here is a favorite with ham:

With a wooden spoon, beat ½ cup packed brown sugar, ¼ cup dry mustard, 1 tbsp. flour, and 2 eggs together until smooth in a small saucepan. Stir in ⅓ cup white vinegar and ⅓ cup water. Set over medium heat and stir until thick.

Makes about 1 cup. Keeps several weeks in the refrigerator.

MEDIUM WHITE SAUCE
▼▼▼

1 tbsp.	butter or margarine
1 tbsp.	flour
	Dash each salt and pepper
½ cup	milk

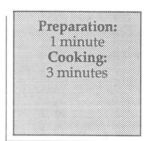

Preparation:
1 minute
Cooking:
3 minutes

Melt butter or margarine in small saucepan over medium heat. Sprinkle in flour, salt, and pepper and stir to blend. Remove from heat and stir in milk all at once. Return to heat and stir until boiling, thickened, and smooth. Reduce heat to low and simmer 2 minutes, stirring.

Makes ½ cup.

VARIATIONS

Cheese Sauce

Add ⅛ tsp. dry mustard with the seasonings and ¼ cup grated old cheddar cheese at the end of the cooking, stirring until cheese is melted.

Mustard Sauce

Stir 1 tbsp. prepared mustard and 1 tsp. prepared horseradish into sauce just before final 2 minutes cooking.

Note: I like Dijon mustard best in this sauce. If you are using hot mustard, use only half the amount.

MUSHROOM SAUCE
▼▼▼

1 tbsp.	butter or margarine
½ cup	sliced mushrooms
2 tsp.	flour
½ cup	chicken stock
	Pinch dried leaf tarragon
	Salt and pepper

Preparation:
3 minutes
Cooking:
10 minutes

Heat butter or margarine in small saucepan. Add mushrooms and cook quickly, stirring, 2 minutes. Sprinkle in flour and stir to blend. Remove from heat and stir in remaining ingredients. Return to medium heat and stir until boiling, thickened, and smooth. Reduce heat to low and simmer 5 minutes, stirring occasionally.

Makes ½ cup.

VARIATIONS

Brown Sauce

Substitute beef stock for chicken stock in above recipe.

Piquant Sauce

Make Brown Sauce omitting mushrooms and tarragon. Instead, stir in 2 tsp. chopped parsley, 2 tsp. chopped dill pickle, and 1 tsp. finely chopped onion along with the beef stock.

TOMATO SAUCE
▼▼▼

1 cup	**canned tomatoes**
¼ tsp.	**garlic salt**
	Grating fresh pepper
½ tsp.	**dried leaf basil**
¼ tsp.	**dried leaf marjoram**

Preparation:
2 minutes
Cooking:
12 minutes

Combine all ingredients in a small saucepan, bring to a boil, breaking up any pieces of tomato. Reduce heat and boil gently 10 minutes.

Makes about 1 cup.

259

TO MAKE GRAVY

Pan Gravy: Remove meat from roasting pan and drain off almost all fat. Leave all the brown bits in the pan. For 1 cup of gravy, sprinkle in 2 tbsp. flour and stir until lightly browned. Remove from heat and add 1 cup of hot liquid gradually, stirring constantly. You can use water or stock. Return to heat and bring to boiling, stirring up all the browned bits from the bottom of the pan. Simmer 2 minutes, season with salt and pepper.

Kettle Gravy: This is the kind of gravy you make for a pot roast. After the meat is removed from the pan, pour the liquid in the pan into a bowl let stand until fat rises to the surface (to speed this up add a few ice cubes), then skim off and discard fat. Add enough water to the liquid remaining to make 2 cups, then return to kettle and heat to boiling. Shake 2 tbsp. flour with ¼ cup cold water in a small jar with a tight lid to blend well, then stir this mixture into the boiling liquid gradually. Boil, stirring, 2 minutes. Season with salt and pepper and a small sprinkling of nutmeg.

INDEX

262

263

266

270

271

273